N

Paula Rego

THE ISLINGTON COOK BOOK

by Islington people

illustrated by local artists

Produced by members of the Islington Branch
of the NSPCC in support of the work being done
to help children in the borough, the City of London
and Tower Hamlets.

First published in Great Britain in 1993

Copyright this recipe collection
© NSPCC Trading Co. Ltd. 1993

Some of the recipes selected by contributors
are taken from published cookery books.
Acknowledgement has been made
wherever possible and we are very
grateful to the original authors.

ISBN 0–902498 54–1

Printed by White Bros. (Printers) Ltd.,
Unit 1, Stockholm Road, London SE16 3LP.

Designed by OMNIFIC STUDIOS

Typeset by AUGUST FILMSETTING
in Monotype Joanna

ACKNOWLEDGEMENTS

The NSPCC gratefully thanks the following for their generous sponsorship of this book, thus enabling the proceeds of its sale to be donated directly to the help of needy children:-

British Petroleum
Arthur Andersen Consulting
Baker Tilly
Barclays de Zoete Wedd
Bircham & Co.
Mr Paul Dacre
Mr & Mrs Simon Hall
John Lewis
Jones Lang Wootton
NatWest Securities
NatWest Ventures
Mr & Mrs Brian Pearse
Mr Michael Pescod
Price Waterhouse
Thames Water

We would also like to thank all those who have contributed recipes; Omnific Studios/London (Derek Birdsall, Martin Lee and Pep Sala) our graphic designers; Margaret Willes our editor; Martin Jones, Sarah Phillips, Clare Thomas (our NSPCC contact) and the artists who have created special illustrations for the book: Stephen Cox, Juliet Lawson, Marianne Fox Ockinga, Wendy Jacob, Mary Kleinmann, Gail Lilly, John Melvin, Paula Rego, Robin Richmond, Pep Sala and Posy Simmonds.

And special thanks are due to two long-suffering husbands, who have actually gone without meals in the interests of this cook book, Brian Palmer and Christopher McCann.

FOREWORD

Anyone who has ever written a book and struggled through the horrors of copy deadlines can think of no more delightful a task than being asked just to write the foreword for someone else's book. No sitting up all night re-reading page proofs, no decisions about typefaces or design, all that is required is a few well chosen words with one's name at the bottom!

No words I can say about the cause this book supports could speak more vividly than the reports that almost daily appear in the newspapers telling of the grim lives so many children and their families live. That we can help ease their troubles by buying such an eclectic, eccentric and energetic collection seems too simple to be true.

This, though, is rather more than just any charity cook book. A collection as wide and far reaching as this is a document cataloguing social history, one that in times to come will enable others to picture Islington as it was in 1993. Who lived there, what they did and what they ate.

For me the book is a sketch of my life in Islington. Names from the past come flooding back with their associated memories. Antonia Dugdale's School of Dancing, where my children stuck as tightly to my skirt as I'm sure her recipe for toffee will stick to your teeth. Mr Edwards of Douglas Pharmacy, whose patent chicken pox anti-itch lotion soothed generations of Islington spots. Will his recipe, also for toffee, be as magical, I wonder?

Most importantly this is a book of wonderful recipes, recipes from every corner of the globe as represented by those who live in Islington. We have recipes from headteachers and historians, police inspectors and publicans, butchers and bankers, architects and The Arsenal. Each has brought its own special flavour to the collection, but each is also about hospitality and generosity.

Is there any more natural or powerful emotion than that of wanting to feed one's family? For eating and sharing meals is surely one of the most fundamental aspects of family life. Buying this book will not only inspire us to feed our families well but will allow other families whose needs are different, but no less important, also to be nourished.

There can be no better cause than the NSPCC and few better cook books than this one. I entreat you to buy not just one copy but many, and give them to friends, neighbours, cousins, aunts and uncles.

Thane Prince
Cookery Editor
The Daily Telegraph

Imperial and metric measurements are given in these recipes.

Tablespoons, dessertspoons and teaspoons are flat not heaped.

When using a fan-assisted oven reduce the cooking time slightly according to the oven cooking instruction booklet, or cook at a slightly lower temperature.

Where we have referred to cups they are assumed to be American measures and we list below the equivalent amounts:-

Oven Temperature Chart:

°C	°F	Gas mark
130	250	slow
140	275	1
150	300	2
170	325	3
180	350	4 moderate
190	375	5
200	400	6 moderately hot
220	425	7 hot
230	450	8
240	475	9 very hot

Liquid Measures:

$\frac{1}{4}$ US cup	= 60 ml =	2 fluid oz
1 US cup	= 240 ml =	8 fluid oz
2 US cups	= 480 ml =	16 fluid oz

Butter/Margarine Measures:

2 level tablespoons =	25g = 1 oz
8 level tablespoons =	100g = 4 oz

Dry Measures:

1 US cup =	25g = 1 oz parsley, chives
1 US cup =	50g = 2 oz crisps, coconut flakes
1 US cup =	25g = 3 oz rolled oats, oatbran, bran flakes, porridge oats
1 US cup =	100g = 4 oz Parmesan cheese, cocoa, chopped almonds, green peppers, onions, frozen vegetables, celery, cubed boiled potatoes, carrots
1 US cup =	125g = 5 oz flour, corn meal
1 US cup =	175g = 6 oz raisins, sultanas
1 US cup =	200g = 7 oz rice, kidney beans, sugar, cubed beef, chicken, canned tomatoes
1 US cup =	225g = 8 oz peanut butter
1 US cup =	350g = 12 oz molasses

SMOKED MACKEREL PATE	12	Francis Golding, ICMS
CRABMEAT MOUSSE	12	Chris Smith, MP, Islington South and Finsbury
SALMON MOUSSE	12	Louise Nicholson, writer and traveller
OEUFS MARIE ANTOINETTE	13	Ketcher and Moore, interior designers
CONSOMME MOUSSE	14	Mary Cosh, Islington historian
CHILLED EGG MIXTURE	14	Marion Harvey, The Islington Society
COLD SCOTCH WOODCOCK	15	David King, actor
CHAMPIGNONS FREDERICK'S	15	Louis Segal, Frederick's Restaurant
AVOCADO CREAMS	16	Doreen Napolitano, Chapel Market stallholder
SMOKED SALMON	16	Griff Rhys Jones, actor
ICED WATERCRESS AND LEMON SOUP	17	Nikki Porter, Sequinpark
LEEK AND POTATO SOUP	17	Bay Hodgson, retired army officer
THREE (OR MORE) MUSHROOM SOUP	18	Martin Lee, Omnific
A TIP FOR PRAWN COCKTAILS	20	Gloria Elliott, James Elliot, Essex Road butchers

SOUPS & STARTERS

FRENCH ONION SOUP	20	Alec Forshaw, Islington's Conservation Officer
MR SMITH'S CELERY SOUP	21	Geoffrey Smith, political journalist
OLD BILL'S BROTH	21	Inspector Clark, Highbury Vale Police Station
ROAST GARLIC AND POTATO SOUP	22	Gill Wing, Le Café
GREEN PEA AND WATERCRESS SOUP	23	Lily Mitchell, antique dealer, Camden Passage
PEANUT SOUP	23	Bob Swash, producer
MUNG SOUP	24	Chuka and Dubem Okonkwo, The Highbury Twins
CULLEN SKINK SOUP	24	Neal Ascherson, The Independent
GAZPACHO	25	Alan Howard, actor
COLD BEETROOT SOUP	26	Caroline Grocholska, NSPCC Committee
PEA AND MINT SOUP	27	Louis Segal, Frederick's Restaurant

SMOKED MACKEREL PATE

Francis Golding, International Council for Monuments and Sites

Skin a whole smoked mackerel (much juicier than fillets) and take the flesh from the bones. Put in food processor with the juice of a lemon, plenty of freshly ground black pepper, a teaspoon of dry English mustard and a dessertspoon of yoghurt. Process until smooth and serve with hot brown toast.

CRABMEAT MOUSSE

Chris Smith, MP, Islington South and Finsbury

$\frac{1}{2}$ can condensed cream of mushroom soup
8 oz/225 g cream cheese
1 envelope unflavoured gelatine
$\frac{1}{8}$ cup water
$\frac{1}{2}$ cup mayonnaise

$\frac{1}{2}$ cup celery, chopped
1 small onion, chopped
7 oz/200 g crabmeat
salt and pepper

Melt the soup and cream cheese over a low heat. Add all the other ingredients including the gelatine dissolved in the water. Chill overnight.

SALMON MOUSSE

Louise Nicholson, writer and traveller

My mother's standby, since the ingredients were always lurking in her chilly, well-stocked, walk-in larder. I've only once seen someone toff their over-sensitive nose at the salmon being tinned and not fresh – the paprika somehow revives it.

1 packet gelatine
1 lb/450 g tinned salmon, drained (unless you have a deluge of fresh salmon)
1 pint/500 ml mayonnaise, using 3 yolks (if really desperate,
    ready-made is OK)
paprika   lemon juice
freshly ground pepper   3 egg whites

Melt the gelatine in warm water. Squish the salmon with a fork, add mayonnaise, gelatine and plenty of seasonings. Fold in thoroughly 2 spoonfuls of the stiffly beaten egg whites, then add the rest. Pour mixture into tin mould (a ring one is especially good but a bread tin will do). Once set, turn out onto serving dish and garnish with slivers of cucumber and, for a splash, one giant prawn per person.

OEUFS MARIE ANTOINETTE

Ketcher and Moore, interior designers

Serves 6

5 medium eggs
1 $\frac{1}{2}$ oz/37 g butter
1 small packet frozen prawns
1 heaped teaspoon/5 ml Dijon mustard
1 tablespoon/15 ml parsley, chopped
1 tablespoon/15 ml chervil, chopped (or 1 teaspoon/5 ml dried chervil)
$\frac{1}{4}$ pint/150 ml single cream
1$\frac{1}{2}$ oz/37 g cheese, finely grated (or breadcrumbs)
salt and pepper
1 oz/25 g butter (for topping)

Boil eggs for approximately 6 minutes, drain and run under cold water, peel and chop fairly coarsely.

Melt the butter in a pan. Add eggs, prawns, mustard, parsley, chervil and cream.

Combine over gentle heat and adjust seasoning.

Pour into 6 buttered ramekin dishes and put into a moderate oven, 375F/190C/gas mark 5, for 15–20 minutes.

Pre-heat grill and put a small knob of butter on each ramekin with the cheese or breadcrumbs and grill until lightly brown.

Serve immediately with toast or warm rolls and chilled white wine.

CONSOMME MOUSSE

Mary Cosh, Islington historian

My contribution is easy to make and exotic to eat, and can – indeed should – be made the day before.

Serves 6

All that is needed to make this starter is a tin of beef consommé beaten up with a carton of cream cheese, with a teaspoon/5 ml of curry powder stirred in. It can be served liquid, in soup bowls, if preferred, but I think it nicer chilled in ramekins, so that it forms a kind of simplified mousse. Chopped parsley sprinkled on top before serving adds to the appearance.

Last time I made this it refused to set, for unexplained reasons. Never mind, the flavour is just as good – just use soup spoons!

CHILLED EGG MIXTURE

Marion Harvey, The Islington Society

Serves 6

This chilled egg mixture, called Farshir Ovannye Jatsa Vskoruipf, is lovely as a first course. The mixture is supposed, for spectacular effect, to be stuffed in the empty shells, cut in half lengthways; I skip that, and serve either in individual ramekins or a glass bowl.

6 eggs, hard-boiled
4–6 canned anchovies, plus 2 for garnish, finely chopped
2 heaped tablespoons/30 ml mayonnaise, or fromage frais, or a mixture of
    both
3 tablespoons/45 ml fresh parsley or dill, finely chopped

Mash the egg whites and yolks, or blend in a food processor to a purée.

Mix the anchovies and add the mayonnaise or fromage frais.

Mix until completely blended.

Chill for several hours.

Garnish with small pieces of anchovy and sprigs of dill or parsley.

COLD SCOTCH WOODCOCK

David King, actor

My favourite starter. A delicious combination of eggs and fish.

Lightly scramble the eggs, (at least 2 per person, and no salt because there are anchovies to follow). When cool, criss-cross the eggs with anchovy fillets. Empty a tin of cold consommé, kept in the fridge until the last moment to make it chunkier, and simply sprinkle with chopped parsley.

Goes down very well with homemade wholemeal bread.

CHAMPIGNONS FREDERICK'S (the original!)

Louis Segal, Frederick's Restaurant

3 oz/75 g small clean button mushrooms
cornflour
salt and pepper
$\frac{1}{2}$ pint/250 ml milk
2 eggs, well whisked and seasoned
natural breadcrumbs, fine
oil
lemon
tartare sauce (or any other dip)

Wipe the mushrooms as necessary.

Roll in cornflour with a touch of seasoning.

Shake well to remove excess – mushrooms should be well dusted all over.

Dip into the mixture of milk and eggs. Drain slightly.

Roll in large quantity of breadcrumbs – mushrooms should be well covered with a fine coat. Deep fry in clean hot oil until golden brown all over – this should only take 1 minute. The mushrooms should be crisp and dry.

Roll onto kitchen roll to remove excess oil.

Serve with a wedge of lemon and tartare sauce.

AVOCADO CREAMS Doreen Napolitano, Chapel Market stallholder

Serves 4

$\frac{1}{4}$ pint/150 ml fresh double cream
1 tablespoon/15 ml wine vinegar
5 anchovy fillets, finely chopped
1 level dessertspoon/10 ml onion, finely chopped
2 level teaspoons/10 ml sugar
2 large ripe avocados (obtainable from Doreen's barrow)
salt
cayenne pepper
paprika to sprinkle over pears
lemon and cucumber slices

Whip cream until thick.

Combine vinegar with anchovies, onions and sugar.

Halve avocados, remove flesh and mash finely; retain the skins.

Combine with cream and vinegar mixture.

Season to taste with salt and cayenne pepper.

Pile back into shells and sprinkle lightly with paprika.

Garnish each half pear with lemon and cucumber slice.

Chill for half an hour.

SMOKED SALMON Griff Rhys Jones, actor

Useful as a starter, a snack or an entire repast.

Go to a reputable sales outlet and purchase a quantity of smoked salmon. It is easily recognisable owing to its alarming pink colour. Usually there is a name on the package saying 'Smoked Salmon'.

Take out of the packet with scissors. Lay daintily on a plate. Sprinkle with lemon juice and pepper according to taste.

Serves 2. In extremis this recipe can serve 4; simply put less on each plate.

ICED WATERCRESS AND LEMON SOUP

Nikki Porter, Sequinpark

2 bunches watercress
1 onion, finely chopped
$\frac{3}{4}$ pint/450 ml white stock (eg chicken stock)
$\frac{1}{2}$ pint/300 ml skimmed milk
rind of 1 lemon, finely grated
salt and pepper
5 oz/150 ml carton natural yoghurt

Wash the watercress and remove excess stalks. Chop leaves roughly, leaving some sprigs for garnish. Put into a pan with the onion, stock, milk, grated lemon rind and seasoning to taste. Simmer gently for 30 minutes. Purée in a blender or pass through a fine sieve and allow to cool. Stir in yoghurt, adjust seasoning and chill.

Serve topped with sprigs of watercress.

LEEK AND POTATO SOUP

Bay Hodgson, retired army officer

4 medium-sized leeks
2 oz/50 g butter or margarine
3 small potatoes
$\frac{1}{4}$ pint/150 ml water
1 pint/500 ml chicken stock

1 teaspoon/5 ml salt
pinch of pepper
$\frac{1}{4}$ pint/150 ml milk
chives or spring onion tops to garnish

Use white part of leeks only; wash well and chop. Melt the butter or margarine in a pan and cook the leeks slowly for 10–15 minutes without letting them brown. Peel potatoes and cut into cubes, add to leeks with water and stock, and bring to the boil. Season and simmer in covered pan for 25 minutes until potatoes are soft. Rub the mixture through a sieve, return to pan, add the milk and heat but do not boil.

Serve hot or cold, sprinkled with chives or onion tops.

THREE (OR MORE) MUSHROOM SOUP

Martin Lee, Omnific

5 oz/150 g each of three different types of mushrooms (button,
   oyster, chestnut; or any combination of different flavoured mushrooms)
2 shallots, or 1 medium onion
1 stick celery
1 medium clove garlic
2–3 chicken livers
1 pint/600 ml chicken stock
$\frac{1}{2}$ teaspoon/2.5 ml dried thyme, more if fresh
$\frac{1}{2}$ teaspoon/2.5 ml dried tarragon, more if fresh
6 black peppercorns, crushed
2 all-spice berries, crushed
salt
2 oz/50 g butter
4 tablespoons/60 ml olive oil
garnishes: milk/cream; chives/parsley; croutons

Chop shallots, garlic and celery finely; cook in the butter and olive oil on a low
heat until onions are translucent. Chop mushrooms coarsely, add and cook for
5 minutes. Chop chicken livers finely and add together with the stock, herbs
and spices and simmer for 20 minutes. Allow to cool sufficiently to liquidise
thoroughly (in Kenwood, or equivalent). This will produce a thick soup.
Reduce to taste with stock/water/or milk, for a creamier soup. Taste and
adjust flavour, if required.

To serve: Reheat, serve with swirl of cream and garnish with chopped chives
or parsley. Croutons help – if you have the time or energy to make them.

This recipe takes about 50 minutes in total, excluding the shopping.

opposite: John Melvin

JOHN MELVIN 92.

A tip for PRAWN COCKTAILS

Gloria Elliott, James Elliott, Essex Road butcher

When making prawn cocktail sauce, add a generous amount of creamed horseradish to taste. This effectively takes away that sickly sweetness and adds a bit of a kick!

FRENCH ONION SOUP

Alec Forshaw, Islington's Conservation Officer

Serves 6

This has been produced by the bucket-load for the annual Christmas lunch in the Planning Department of Islington Council, and usually goes down well as a starter. It also has the distinct advantage of being able to be made the night before and heated up the following day with no adverse results.

5 large onions
6 oz/170 g butter
1 teaspoon/5 ml thyme
2 pints/1.25 litres clear potato broth (or 4 vegetable stock cubes dissolved in 2 pints/1.25 litres water)
1 tablespoon/15 ml lemon juice
salt and pepper
2 tablespoons/30 ml brandy or dry sherry
6 slices French bread
$\frac{1}{2}$ lb/225 g Gruyère cheese, finely grated

Chop the onions, not too fine, and gently sauté them in the butter together with the thyme in a large pan until soft and brown. Do not allow to burn. Add the potato broth (made by boiling potato peelings, 2 carrots and a stick of celery in water). Add the lemon juice, salt and pepper, and brandy or sherry. Cover the pan and simmer for $\frac{1}{2}$ hour, so that the liquid does not reduce. Serve in flattish bowls and top each portion with a thin slice of toasted French bread, liberally sprinkled with finely grated Gruyère cheese. As a short-cut, use a packet of Melba toasts; they go a bit soggy, but it's easy, especially if you don't have a toaster in the office!

MR SMITH'S CELERY SOUP

Geoffrey Smith, political journalist

butter for frying
8 oz/225 g celery, chopped
1 medium onion, peeled and finely chopped
1 clove garlic, chopped

1 tablespoon/15 ml flour
2 pints/1.25 litre chicken stock
salt and pepper to taste

Melt butter in saucepan and add celery, onion and garlic. Cook gently for 5 minutes. Stir in flour and continue cooking for 1 minute, stirring constantly. Gradually add the stock and bring to the boil. Add salt and pepper, and lower heat, half cover and simmer gently for 20 minutes. Purée in blender or food processor, return to rinsed-out pan and reheat.

OLD BILL'S BROTH

Inspector Clark, Highbury Vale Police Station

2 large carrots
2 large parsnips
2 large onions
1 oz/25 g pearl barley
1 oz/25 g split red lentils

14oz/400 g can Italian tomatoes
1 teaspoon/5 ml dried mixed herbs
salt and black pepper, freshly milled
2½ pints/1.5 litres vegetable stock

Garnish:
2 oz/50 g strong matured Cheddar cheese, grated
6 slices French bread

Place the carrots, parsnips, onions, barley, lentils and tomatoes in a large flame-proof casserole, sprinkle in the herbs, season with the salt and pepper, and pour in the stock. Bring everything up to simmering point. Then put on a lid, keep the heat very low and simmer the soup for about 2 hours.

About 5 minutes before serving, pre-heat the grill to its highest setting. Sprinkle the cheese over the slices of French bread and lay them on the surface of the soup. Now place the casserole under the hot grill until the cheese has melted and become bubbly and brown.

ROAST GARLIC AND POTATO SOUP

Gill Wing, Le Café

Although this recipe contains whole bulbs of garlic, pre-roasting the cloves in their outer skin gives a very subtle flavour to the finished soup.

2 bulbs garlic, cloves separated but skin left on

2 oz/50 g olive oil

2 oz/50 g butter

4 oz/125 g onion, sliced

4 oz/125 g leek, sliced

1 lb/450 g potatoes, peeled and diced

1½ pints/750 ml vegetable stock

¼ pint/150 ml dry white wine

salt

black pepper, freshly ground

nutmeg, freshly ground

¼ pint/150 ml double cream

Place garlic and olive oil in a roasting tin and cook in oven at 400F/200C/gas mark 6 for 30–40 minutes, until golden brown.

Sauté the onion and leek in the butter in a saucepan for 5–10 minutes until golden brown.

Add potatoes, stock and wine and cook for 30 minutes.

Add pre-roasted garlic and oil, and cook for another 30 minutes. A little more stock may be needed at this stage, depending on evaporation.

Remove from heat and liquidise, then pass through a fine sieve. This will remove the outer skin from the cloves of garlic.

Bring the soup back to the boil and add salt, pepper and nutmeg to taste.

The double cream is added just before serving – and the soup reheated.

If you are garlic mad, garlic-flavoured croutons make a suitable accompaniment.

GREEN PEA AND WATERCRESS SOUP

Lily Mitchell, antique dealer, Camden Passage

1 large onion, roughly chopped
1 tablespoon/15 ml olive oil or butter
1½ pints/750 ml water
1 vegetable or chicken stock cube
12 oz/350 g frozen garden peas
1 large bunch watercress, chopped
3 twists of the pepper mill
single cream to garnish

Soften the onion in oil or butter. Add the water and stock cube and bring to the boil. Add the peas, watercress and pepper and simmer gently for 15 minutes. Liquidise to a thick smooth soup, season to taste and serve with swirls of single cream. If you prefer a sharper taste, increase the watercress.

PEANUT SOUP

Bob Swash, producer

2 cups onion, chopped
1 tablespoon/15 ml peanut or soya oil
½ teaspoon/2.5 ml cayenne
1 teaspoon/5 ml fresh ginger, grated
1 cup carrots, chopped
2 cups sweet potatoes, chopped
4 cups vegetable stock
1 cup smooth peanut butter
2 cups tomato juice
1 cup chives, chopped

Sauté onion in oil until clear. Add cayenne, ginger and then the carrots, the potatoes and stock. Simmer for 15 minutes. Purée and return to pot. Add peanut butter, stirring until smooth. Reheat, stirring to prevent sticking, and add tomato juice. Chopped chives should be sprinkled over each bowl of soup.

MUNG SOUP

Chuka and Dubem Okonkwo, The Highbury Twins

8 oz/225 g mung beans
½ oz/15 g wakame
½ oz/15 g dulse

1 tablespoon/15 ml miso
salt and pepper

Soak mung beans overnight. The following day soak the wakame and the dulse separately in a pint/500 ml of water for 30 minutes. Cook the beans with the sea vegetables in 2 pints/1.25 litres water for around 12–15 minutes. Once cooked, blend and return to cooker, warming for a further 10 minutes over a gentle flame. Add miso and salt and pepper if required before serving.

Sea vegetables tend to have a high salt content. Further addition of salt is not healthy for anyone suffering from high blood pressure.

CULLEN SKINK SOUP

Neal Ascherson, The Independent

1 leek
1 tablespoon/15 g butter
2 pieces smoked haddock
1 tablespoon/15 ml flour
1 potato
1 bay leaf
½ pint/300 ml water
½ pint/300 ml milk
seasoning to taste
parsley

Chop up white of leek, soften in butter. Add floured haddock in small pieces, diced potato, bay leaf and water.

Bring to the boil. Simmer for 20 minutes. Add milk and heat (not boiling). Blend, if wished. Season, adding chopped parsley.

GAZPACHO

Alan Howard, actor

Serves 4–6

This is an adaptation of Margaret Costa's recipe in her excellent *Four Seasons Cookery Book*. It is marvellously refreshing for lunch on a hot summer's day – and it has one great advantage, it can be prepared by people who, like me, cannot cook....

4 thick slices good (stale) bread
2 dessertspoons/20 ml red wine vinegar
2 cloves garlic, crushed
4 tablespoons/60 ml good olive oil
$1\frac{1}{2}$ lb/675 g large tomatoes, skinned
1 large Spanish onion, very finely chopped
$\frac{1}{2}$ cucumber, very finely chopped
2 red peppers, very finely chopped
15 oz/450 ml jar tomato juice
salt and black pepper
garnishes, see below

Use bread to make fine breadcrumbs. Stir in the vinegar and crushed garlic. Add the olive oil slowly. Chop the tomatoes to a fine pulp. Chop very finely the onion, cucumber and red peppers. Add these ingredients, and the tomato juice to the oil/vinegar/breadcrumb mixture. Blend in blender or food processor until completely smooth. Add pepper and salt to taste. Dilute carefully with iced water until the soup has a thin, creamy consistency, but retains its bite. Chill.

The soup is improved by standing, and the preparation to this point may be made the day before serving; certainly allow the soup to chill for 3–4 hours.

Before serving, prepare the following garnishes, all finely diced: cucumber, red peppers, skinned fresh tomatoes, small diced croutons of bread fried in olive oil. Very finely sliced sweet Spanish onions may also be used as garnish.

Serve these with the soup, the garnishes making its consistency thick – a kind of salad soup.

COLD BEETROOT SOUP (CHLODNIK)

Caroline Grocholska, NSPCC Committee

Soup features strongly in Polish households. Often conceived as a main meal they are wholesome, filling and sustaining to provide warmth and nourishment during the freezing winter months. In the summer cold soups are very popular, sometimes made of fruit or of cucumber or beetroot. This Lithuanian beetroot soup is very easy to make, tastes delicious and looks very pretty with the green flecks of the dill and chives standing out against the delicate pink background.

Serves 4

$\frac{1}{2}$ pint/300 ml beet juice, obtained from boiling the peeled beetroot in water
$\frac{1}{2}$ pint/300 ml sour cream
$\frac{3}{4}$ pint/450 ml natural yoghurt
1 cucumber, peeled and chopped
2 tablespoons/30 ml fresh dill, chopped
a little finely grated raw beetroot (just to add colour)
2 tablespoons/30 ml fresh chives, chopped
4 medium-sized radishes, thinly sliced
1 hard-boiled egg

Combine all the ingredients, except the egg, and chill in the refrigerator for at least 4 hours before serving, to let the flavours mingle. Just before serving, quarter or slice the hard-boiled egg and arrange it in the soup plates, pour the soup over and serve.

PEA AND MINT SOUP

Louis Segal, Frederick's Restaurant

1 large leek, sliced and well washed	1 lb/450 g fresh or frozen peas
1 large onion, sliced	bay leaf
4 oz/125 g butter	salt and pepper
2 pints/1.25 litres chicken stock	8 fl oz/240 ml double cream
2 large baking potatoes, peeled and diced	fresh mint

Gently fry the leek and onion in half the butter until soft and transparent but without coloration. Add chicken stock, potatoes, peas, bay leaf, salt and pepper. Simmer gently for 15 minutes. Remove bay leaf. Add cream, fresh mint (10 leaves) and remaining butter and liquidise straight away. Check seasoning. Serve with a sprig of mint.

Natural yoghurt can be substituted for cream.

TOMATO HERB SALAD	30	Lady Olga Maitland, MP, Sutton and Cheam.
BEETROOT AND WALNUT SALAD	30	Marion Harvey, The Islington Society
BRAISED ENDIVE	30	Anthony Delarue, architect
GOAT'S CHEESE AND BACON SALAD	31	Melanie Paine, interior decorator, partner in Paine & Co.
SALADE CUITE	32	Jean Engel, specialist in Moroccan rugs
CHRISTMAS SALAD	32	Glenda Weil, NSPCC Committee
HERBY VINAIGRETTE DRESSING	33	Tom and Gerry Mannion, actors
FAVOURITE PEA RECIPES	33	John R G Murray, publisher
HOMEMADE BAKED BEANS	34	Alan Watkins, The Observer
SLIMMER'S FRENCH DRESSING	35	Nikki Porter, Sequinpark

SALADS & VEGETABLES

CELERIAC AND POTATO   35   Stephen Bull, restaurateur
GRATIN DAUPHINOIS

SWEET AND SOUR CABBAGE   36   Jane Tuely, artist

DANDUL   36   Rupert Perry, Islington Councillor
                       and finalist in the 1988 Observer cookery
                       competition

CELERIAC REMOULADE   37   Dr Lenka Speight, GP

WEST INDIAN RICE AND BEANS   37   Diane Abbott, MP, Hackney North
                                    & Stoke Newington

AUBERGINES AND TOMATOES   38   Linda Binnington, marital psychotherapist

PATATAS A LA IMPORTANTE   39   The Continental Touch,
                                    Spanish delicatessen

TOMATO HERB SALAD Lady Olga Maitland, MP, Sutton and Cheam

Serves 6

3 lbs/1.5 kg small firm tomatoes
large handful fresh herbs (parsley, mint, coriander, marjoram, thyme)
3 fat garlic cloves
dressing

Slice the tomatoes. Roughly chop the herbs (not in a Magimix, by hand) and the garlic. Into a pretty glass bowl, lay a layer of tomatoes, then herbs, season and repeat until complete. Wrap in cling film and leave in fridge for several hours. Before serving, make a generous cup of vinaigrette which has a touch of sugar.

Serve with plenty of fresh crusty bread to mop up the juices.

BEETROOT AND WALNUT SALAD

Marion Harvey, The Islington Society

A most unusual mixture if you like garlic is Salat Svyokly's Orekham/Beetroot and Walnut Salad.

8 oz/225 g cooked beetroot, peeled and chopped
3 oz/75 g walnuts, finely chopped
2 cloves garlic, finely chopped
3 tablespoons/45 ml mayonnaise, or smetana, or sour cream
walnut halves, to garnish

Mix together all the ingredients, or purée in a food processor. Chill for 3 hours, or better still, leave overnight. Serve in a bowl decorated with walnut halves.

BRAISED ENDIVE (Chicory) Anthony Delarue, architect

One or two heads per person, depending on size.

Cut into halves or quarters, melt a little butter in a thick pan and put the endive in. Sprinkle with a few drops of lemon juice to keep it white, and a little salt. Cover and braise slowly until cooked, about ½ hour.

GOAT'S CHEESE AND BACON SALAD

Melanie Paine, interior decorator, partner in Paine & Co.

Frankly, I am a completely hopeless cook – disorganised and not very good at it! Salads, though, I love – both to prepare and to eat – and this one is a favourite.

Prepare individual plates rather than one huge bowl.

Per person:
2 rashers smoked bacon, chopped
juice of $2\frac{1}{2}$ oranges
good few handfuls of green salad
   (use leafy lettuce, curly endive, frisé, cos, etc.)
1–2 rounds (depending on size) goat's cheese

Dressing:
$\frac{1}{3}$ balsamic vinegar
$\frac{2}{3}$ oil (mix olive with vegetable or sunflower, so not too rich)
juice of $\frac{1}{2}$ orange
$\frac{1}{2}$ teaspoon/2.5 ml English mustard
pinch sugar
salt and pepper
1 clove garlic, crushed

Toss chopped bacon in frying pan in its own fat for a couple of minutes and then add orange juice. Simmer over low heat for 10 minutes or so, stirring frequently.

Prepare green salad and place in bowls.

Prepare dressing by mixing all ingredients together and shaking well.

Lightly grill the goat's cheese so that it is warmed and slightly melting.

Remove bacon from heat and add to green salad.

Pour over dressing as required.

Place goat's cheese on top of salad.

SALADE CUITE Jean Engel, specialist in Moroccan rugs

A standard Moroccan dish for the beginning of the meal.

Serves 8–10

4 lbs/2 kg tomatoes, very ripe, peeled, seeded and chopped
1½ lbs/675 g green peppers, roasted, peeled and chopped
2 cloves garlic
paprika, cayenne pepper and salt to taste

Fry the tomatoes in oil, reducing the liquid. Add the green peppers, garlic, paprika, cayenne pepper and salt to taste, and reduce gently until thick. Be careful to stir them to avoid burning. Drain if necessary and serve lukewarm or cool with bread.

CHRISTMAS SALAD Glenda Weil, NSPCC Committee

Serves 6–8

1 clove garlic, peeled
1 large, or 2 small, heads radicchio
2 spears chicory
1 bunch watercress
1 crisp Cox's apple
2 tablespoons/30 ml pecans or walnuts, shelled and coarsely chopped

Dressing:
4 tablespoons/60 ml peanut oil
2 tablespoons/30 ml walnut oil
1–1½ tablespoons/15–20 ml raspberry vinegar
salt and freshly ground black pepper

Rub the salad bowl with garlic and discard the clove.

Tear any large leaves of radicchio into two or three pieces and put all the radicchio in the bowl, together with the separated leaves of chicory and top sprigs of watercress. Quarter and core the apple and cut into thin moon-shaped slivers, with or without the skin. Add these to the salad together with the nuts. Mix all the dressing ingredients together and pour over the salad. Toss well and serve immediately.

HERBY VINAIGRETTE DRESSING

Tom and Gerry Mannion, actors

6 tablespoons/90 ml olive oil
2 tablespoons/30 ml wine vinegar
$\frac{1}{2}$ teaspoon/3 ml whole grain mustard
1 clove garlic, finely chopped
2 teaspoon/10 ml oregano
3 teaspoons/15 ml white sugar
salt and freshly milled black pepper

Beat the oil and vinegar together with the mustard and herbs. Add the garlic, sugar, salt and pepper and continue to stir until well mixed. Pour into a screw top jar and store in fridge. Use within 2 days. Shake thoroughly before use.

FAVOURITE PEA RECIPES John R G Murray, publisher

With full acknowledgement to Janet Ross and Michael Waterfield's delightful *Leaves from our Tuscan Kitchen*.

Serves 6

PISELLI ALLA FRANCESE:

Put a 2-pint/1.25 litre jug full of shelled peas in a saucepan with 2 chopped lettuces and 1 chopped onion and stew in butter, adding salt and pepper, to taste, and 2 cups of good stock. Cook over a good heat stirring all the time.

PISELLI ALL BORGHESE:

Shell enough peas to fill a 2-pint/1.25 litre jug. Meanwhile cook 1 onion, finely chopped, and 2 chopped slices of ham gently in 2 oz/50 g of butter. Add the peas, a bunch of herbs, salt and pepper, plus 2 cups of good stock. Boil fiercely until cooked and the liquid has reduced.

If fresh garden peas are not available (they are always the best), frozen petit pois can be used.

Motto: 'The simpler the recipe, the more delicious the meal!'

HOMEMADE BAKED BEANS

Alan Watkins, The Observer

1 lb/450 g haricot or canelli beans (make sure that the beans have not been
   hanging about in the shop; a dusty packet is an indication that they have
   been. Cypriot or Italian shops tend to have a high turnover.)
1 tin tomatoes
1 medium onion
2 cloves garlic
olive oil
3 medium rashers smoked streaky bacon (ordinary packet stuff will do unless
   you have access to a proper bacon supplier – the best choice is Italian
   panchetta)
1 teaspoon/5 ml sweet paprika
1 teaspoon/5 ml dried thyme
$\frac{1}{2}$ teaspoon/2.5 ml sugar
tomato purée
salt and ground black pepper
1 glass red wine (optional)

Soak beans in plenty of cold water overnight.

Next day, bring beans to boil in cold water. Do not add salt. Skim, cover and
simmer for 35 minutes, or until beans are soft. Drain in colander.

While beans are cooking, gently fry in oil in heavy metal-bottomed casserole
the chopped onion, the first chopped clove of garlic and bacon cut into
$\frac{1}{4}''$ (6 mm) strips. Do not brown. This takes about 15 minutes.

Combine in heavy metal saucepan the oil, second chopped clove of garlic, tin
of tomatoes, tomato paste, thyme, sugar, paprika, salt and pepper. Simmer
with lid for 30 minutes. Allow to settle for 1–2 hours and liquidise or
preferably – to get rid of the pips – sieve through a Moulinex. This sauce can
be made the previous day, when the beans are put in to soak.

Combine cooked beans and sauce with bacon, etc., in heavy casserole. Add
water and red wine just to cover mixture. Cook gently, covered, on top of
stove for $\frac{1}{2}$ hour. Check seasoning. Leave until bedtime. Most of the liquid will
have been absorbed. Add more water. Leave overnight. Check liquid again and
cook in a low oven for 1–2 hours.

SLIMMERS' FRENCH DRESSING

Nikki Porter, Sequinpark

8 fl oz/225 g tomato juice
$\frac{1}{4}$ teaspoon/1 ml celery salt
1 teaspoon/5 ml lemon juice
1 teaspoon/5 ml onion, very finely chopped
$\frac{1}{4}$ teaspoon/1 ml Worcester sauce
$\frac{1}{4}$ teaspoon/1 ml prepared horseradish
1 clove garlic, crushed
salt and freshly ground black pepper

Place all the ingredients together in a small screw-top jar and shake well.
Store in fridge and shake before serving.

CELERIAC AND POTATO GRATIN DAUPHINOIS

Stephen Bull, restaurateur

1 small celeriac (about 2 lb/900g)
1 lb/450 g large potatoes
$\frac{1}{2}$ pint/250 ml milk
$\frac{1}{2}$ pint/250 ml double cream
1 clove garlic, crushed
ground nutmeg
2 oz/50 g Gruyère cheese, grated
salt and pepper

Peel celeriac and potatoes and cut into $\frac{1}{4}$'(6mm) slices.

Bring milk, cream, garlic and nutmeg to the boil.

Place potato and celeriac slices in the liquid.

Bring back to the boil, then put to one side for 15 minutes, or until cool
enough to handle.

In a tray at least 2″(5 cm) high make layers, putting cheese, salt and pepper
between each layer until all potato and celeriac slices are used, finishing with
a layer of cheese on the top.

SWEET AND SOUR CABBAGE Jane Tuely, artist

1 white cabbage, medium-size	3 fresh tomatoes, skinned and chopped
1 large onion	1 tablespoon/15 ml wine vinegar
2 tablespoons/30 ml olive oil	salt and pepper to taste

Chop cabbage finely. Blanch for 2–3 minutes in boiling water. Drain well.
Soften chopped onions in olive oil, add tomatoes and cabbage, vinegar, salt
and pepper. Cook gently, stirring from time to time, for 10 minutes, until
cabbage is cooked.

This cabbage has the great merit that it can be re-heated (even the next day)
with no ill-effects at all.

DANDUL

Rupert Perry, Islington Councillor and finalist in the 1988 Observer cookery
competition

Instead of throwing away the cauliflower leaves, this Indian dish is an ideal
way of using them and it tastes great. If you pretend you want the leaves to
feed your pet rabbit, you can usually get more than enough for free.

2 onions	2 tablespoons/30 ml oil
small piece ginger	salt
2 green chillies	2 lbs/900 g cauliflower leaves and stalks
1 teaspoon/5 ml ground turmeric	1 lemon
1 teaspoon/5 ml ground coriander	

Chop onions, fry with chopped ginger and chopped chillies, until soft.
Add turmeric and coriander and fry for 2 minutes. Add the finely chopped
cauliflower leaves and stalks and fry for 2 minutes. Cover with salted water
and simmer slowly until soft (minimum 1 hour, sometimes 2 hours).

Just before serving add the juice of the lemon. Serve with rice.

Dandul tastes good with most other vegetable or meat curries.

CELERIAC REMOULADE Dr Lenka Speight, GP

Use as a starter or light summer picnic lunch (though difficult to buy a good quality celeriac in the summer).

Peel celeriac. Finely grate (only the firm parts of the root). Mix into a good quality (preferably home-made) mayonnaise. Sprinkle a few drops of freshly squeezed lemon juice over. Season with salt and pepper. Cool in fridge for 1 hour, prior to serving.

Serve with fresh French bread and butter.

WEST INDIAN RICE AND BEANS

Diane Abbott, MP, Hackney North & Stoke Newington

$\frac{1}{2}$ cup red kidney beans
2 oz/50 g coconut cream
salt and pepper
thyme
1 cup white long grain rice

Leave red kidney beans to soak overnight.

Boil until soft; drain.

Measure out 2 cups of water and pour into saucepan.

Add coconut cream, pinch of salt, dash of pepper and thyme.

Add 1 cup of rice.

Cook rice until tender.

AUBERGINES AND TOMATOES

Linda Binnington, marital psychotherapist

Serves 4

2–3 largish aubergines
salt
olive oil
2–3 largish onions
2 14 oz/400 g tins tomatoes, chopped
2 tablespoons/30 ml fresh parsley, chopped
2 tablespoons/30 ml breadcrumbs
grated cheese (preferably Gruyère)
pinch of mixed herbs (optional)

Slice and lay out the aubergines sprinkled with salt. Leave to sweat for about 30 minutes, then rinse and squeeze or pat dry.

Meanwhile, chop and gently fry the onions in oil for a couple of minutes, then add the chopped tomatoes and simmer for about 30 minutes, adding chopped parsley just before the end.

Fry the aubergines in olive oil, cover with the tomato sauce, then sprinkle with breadcrumbs and grated cheese and a pinch of mixed dry herbs if you wish.

Brown under the grill or in top of a hot oven.

Alternatively, this dish can be done in advance and heated through in the oven.

PATATAS ALA IMPORTANTE (POTATOES OF IMPORTANCE) The Continental Touch, Spanish delicatessen

3 lb/1½ kg potatoes
1 tablespoon/15 ml flour
2 eggs
1 small onion

1 small glass white wine
1 pint/500 ml stock
salt, oil

Peel potatoes and slice ¼″(6 mm) thick, sprinkle with salt. Coat them first with flour then with the beaten egg, and fry gently in plenty of oil. Drain and arrange in an oven-proof dish. Fry the onion, add 1 tablespoon/15 ml flour, the wine and the stock. Pour over the potatoes and cook gently in oven for about 15–20 minutes.

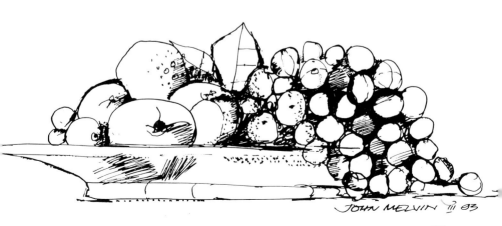

JOHN MELVIN 'III 83

PASTA WITH A RAW TOMATO SAUCE 42 Jonathan Hyde, actor

SPINACH WITH BLUE CHEESE 42 Nigel Slater, cookery writer
AND PASTA

ALL-PURPOSE ITALIAN SAUCE 43 Michael Rosen, children's writer

ROCKET AND CHILLI PASTA 44 Rupert Perry, Islington Councillor
and finalist, 1988 Observer
cookery competition

PESTO ALLA GENOVESE 44 Robert Fox, The Daily Telegraph

SAUTED GREENS, GOAT CHEESE AND 45 The Eagle Pub, Farringdon Road
OLIVES WITH PENNE

FOUR CHEESES PASTA 45 Simon Rattle, conductor and
Elise Ross, opera singer

FISH PASTA 46 Susan Ignatieff, film critic

PRAWNS AND PASTA 46 Gail Lilley, artist, and Rt. Hon.
Peter Lilley, MP, St Albans

PASTA

SICILIAN CAULIFLOWER SAUCE WITH BUCATINI	48	The Eagle Pub, Farringdon Road
SQUID SALAD WITH PASTA	48	Annie Williams, artist
LASAGNETTE VENEZIANA	49	The Portofino and Aqualino's Bar
TAGLIATELLE WITH GRILLED MEDITERRANEAN VEGETABLES	50	Wendy Jacob, artist
PASTA IN AUBERGINE SAUCE	52	Guido Pontecorvo, former Professor of Genetics
PASTA WITH SUN-DRIED TOMATOES	52	Tony Blair, MP, Sedgefield
FERRARI'S PASTA AL CARCIOLI	53	Alimentari Ferrari, delicatessen
VEGETABLE PASTA	53	Chief Superintendent W.G. Sinclair, Metropolitan Police and Scotland Yard

PASTA WITH A RAW TOMATO SAUCE

Jonathan Hyde, actor

Serves 6

6 medium fresh tomatoes (plum tomatoes are excellent)
bunch fresh basil
bunch fresh parsley (Cyprus is excellent)
4 cloves garlic
$1\frac{3}{4}$ lb/750 g long pasta
6 tablespoons/90 ml olive oil
fresh Parmesan cheese

Finely chop tomatoes, herbs and garlic. Season with salt and pepper, and set aside on a large dish.

Boil a large pot of salted water; throw in the long pasta and stir constantly.

Minutes before the pasta is ready, heat the olive oil in a small pan (do not allow to smoke, but it must be very hot).

Drain the pasta.

Pour the oil over the tomatoes, basil, garlic and parsley.

Pour the pasta over and mix vigorously.

Serve immediately with Parmesan cheese.

SPINACH WITH BLUE CHEESE AND PASTA

Nigel Slater, cookery writer

Serves 2

Any soft blue-veined cheese will be right for this. Try Irish Cashel Blue, or Italian Dolcelatte or Gorgonzola. I like to follow this rich and almost instant dish with a plate of salad leaves to mop up the cheesy sauce.

10 oz/275 g fresh pasta, any curled or ribbon shape
2 double handfuls of spinach leaves, washed and torn up

6 oz/175 g soft, blue cheese, cut into cubes
$\frac{1}{2}$ pint/300 ml single cream
salt and freshly ground black pepper

Cook the pasta, uncovered, in salted boiling water until it is tender but firm – about 2 minutes for fresh, 9 minutes for dried. Remember that ribbon pasta cooks very quickly. It should be slightly tacky when cooked, not soggy.

Put the spinach, still wet from washing, in a pan over a medium heat. Cover with a lid, and cook until it starts to wilt, a matter of 2 minutes or so. Add the blue cheese and the cream. Cook over a gentle heat until the cheese melts into the cream. Taste it and season accordingly, remembering that some blue cheeses are quite salty.

When the cheese has melted and the spinach is still bright green, drain the pasta and fold it into the sauce. Eat hot.

ALL-PURPOSE ITALIAN SAUCE

Michael Rosen, children's writer

You can mix this with anything. It tastes brilliant.

Cover the bottom of a pan or casserole dish with about 4 tablespoons/60 ml of very good olive oil. Heat and put in a clove or two of garlic, crushed or squashed, and $\frac{1}{2}$ teaspoon/2.5 ml thyme. Fry for about 3–4 minutes, then add a tin of tomatoes (you will probably need the 2 lb/900 g size). Then, if you have one, use one of those tools that you mash the potatoes up with, I can't think of the name of it, just let's call it a potato masher. Mash the tomatoes into almost a purée. Then add a pinch of oregano, a pinch of basil and a bay leaf or two and then take a lemon and grate a bit of the lemon peel (just a few little pieces) into the sauce. Cook for about 20 minutes and this gives you an Italian sauce that you can add to almost anything.

I like it on any kind of pasta. Then you can grate cheese onto it or you can add something like chick peas, or beans, or anything else that you think is nice. You can pour it onto something like broccoli as well.

ROCKET AND CHILLI PASTA

Rupert Perry, Islington Councillor and finalist, 1988 Observer Cookery competition.

1 lb/500 g pasta shells, bow or twists
8 oz/250 g rocket (usually on sale in Chapel Market or easily grown from seed)
    or spinach, or other green leaves if rocket not available.
3 tablespoons/45 ml olive oil
2/3 cloves of garlic (to taste)
2/3 fresh red chillis (to taste) – green chillis will do
Parmesan cheese
black pepper

Cook pasta in boiling salted water (12 minutes) then drain. Meanwhile, cook rocket in boiling water for 3 minutes, then drain. Heat olive oil in pan and add garlic and chillis, finely chopped. When garlic begins to brown, turn off heat and add pasta and rocket. Toss.

Delicious with Parmesan cheese and black pepper.

PESTO ALLA GENOVESE

Robert Fox, The Daily Telegraph

I first really encountered Pesto alla Genovese in the summer of 1976, through a fear of earthquake, mild revolution and the growing shadow of the Red Brigades in Italy. In Rome spaghetti al pesto was the *piatto del memento* – I seemed to live on it and nothing else. Later I worked on papers in Milan and Genoa, the true home of this marvellous creation. The Genovese pesto has just the right sharpness about it – a bit *piccante*, like the character of the people of Columbus' home port.

Pesto Basil Sauce:

Mash fresh basil leaves in a mortar with 1 or 2 cloves of garlic and a pinch of salt. Add 1 oz/25 g of pine nuts and 1 oz/25 g grated Parmesan or Sardinian pecorino cheese. Beat in olive oil (about a cupful) very slowly until well blended. Enough for 1 lb/450 g of cooked spaghetti.

SAUTEED GREENS, GOAT CHEESE AND OLIVES WITH PENNE

The Eagle Pub, Farringdon Road

1 packet penne pasta
4 tablespoons/50 ml good, flavoured olive oil
4 cloves of garlic, finely chopped
3–4 lb/1.25–1.75 kg mixed greens, such as spinach, swiss chard, green cabbage
  leaves, rocket, strong lettuce etc., washed, dried and roughly shredded
salt and pepper
squeeze of lemon
12 oz/300 g soft fresh goat cheese (unmatured)
about 2 oz/50 ml strong black olives, stoned

Cook the pasta in a large pan of salted and oiled water until 'al dente'.

Heat the oil in a large frying pan or wok. Add the garlic and then the greens as the garlic begins to brown. Toss and stir vigorously for a minute or two – add salt, pepper and a squeeze of lemon. Stir in the pasta, goat cheese and olives until mixed well.

You may want to serve some grated Parmesan alongside.

FOUR CHEESES PASTA

Simon Rattle, conductor and Elise Ross, opera singer

Serves 4

1–1$\frac{1}{2}$ packets of dried spaghetti
butter
$\frac{1}{2}$ cup crème fraîche or single cream
$\frac{1}{2}$ cup fresh Parmesan, grated
$\frac{1}{2}$ cup fontina, grated
approximately 2 oz/50 g Gorgonzola, cut into tiny pieces
approximately 2 oz/50 g another cheese (eg Gouda, Cheddar or bel paese)
  cut or grated
pinch nutmeg
freshly ground black pepper

Cook pasta as usual.

Heat small nob of butter in frying pan.

Add crème fraîche or cream. Add cheeses, slowly stirring constantly until the mixture is thoroughly heated and of a smooth consistency. Add a pinch of nutmeg and black pepper to taste.

Serve immediately over spaghetti.

Cholesterol heaven!

FISH PASTA Susan Ignatieff, film critic

1 large red pepper, quartered	Mediterranean shrimps (1 per person)
pasta (fuseli is best for this)	loads of garlic, chopped
loads of olive oil	coriander, chopped fine
1 lb/450 g shrimps, peeled	salt and black pepper
scallops (1 per person)	Parmesan cheese, freshly grated

Bake red peppers in oven, or under grill, until nearly black, remove skins if possible, and cut into thin strips. Keep hot.

Put pasta to cook, add some olive oil to the boiling water. Sauté all the fish and garlic together in generous amounts of olive oil (otherwise the dish will be too dry), for just a few minutes. Put pasta in large shallow dish, heap everything (fish, peppers and lastly coriander) on top with lots of black pepper and Parmesan cheese. Toss gently at the table.

This dish is very quickly cooked on the spot if all the ingredients have been prepared beforehand. And it is easy and fun to make. And looks lovely!

PRAWNS AND PASTA

Gail Lilley, artist and Rt. Hon. Peter Lilley, MP, St Albans

Don't even think of trying this unless you enjoy seriously spicy food. We make it as an antidote to five weeks of bland, creamy Normandy cuisine.

Serves 2

8 oz/225 g linguine or spaghetti
fruity olive oil
8 large cloves of garlic, peeled and chopped

2 teaspoons/10 ml crushed chillis or 1 heaped teaspoon/7.5 ml Birds
  Eye chillis*, soaked and finely chopped
1 dessertspoon/10 ml Ikan Bilis granules** (fish stock) mixed into $\frac{3}{4}$ teacup
  of hot water
12–16 uncooked King prawns***
fresh coriander

Cook pasta in boiling salted water until slightly underdone. Drain well.

Cover base of heavy frying pan with a layer of olive oil and gently sauté half
the given amount of garlic and chilli for 2–3 minutes. At the same time, do
the same with more oil and the remaining garlic and chilli in the pasta pan.

Add pasta to pan with the hot fish stock and cook gently, uncovered, turning
and stirring for about 3–4 minutes.

Put prawns into frying pan and sauté for 4–5 minutes, turning to coat with
chilli mixture.

Put pasta into warm serving dish. Lay prawns on top and sprinkle with
chopped coriander leaves.

This is messy to eat, particularly if you have not split the prawns, so it is best
served on informal occasions or with finger bowls!

* Chillis (Malawi) – selection available from the foreign food stores in
Blackstock Road.

** Ikan Bilis (Indonesian) – Maggi Ikan Bilis fish stock granules in jars from
Nickel and Dime, Upper Street.

*** King prawns, uncooked and frozen, from Steve Hatt in Essex Road. Fresh
uncooked Gulf prawns are sometimes available.

Gail Lilley

SICILIAN CAULIFLOWER SAUCE WITH BUCATINI

The Eagle Pub, Farringdon Road

1 large cauliflower (if you can find the green Italian variety, all the better),
    cut into quarters, leaving all but the toughest leaves intact
2 medium onions, sliced thinly
2 cloves garlic, chopped
2 tablespoons/30 ml currants or raisins, soaked until plump
extra virgin olive oil
a generous pinch of saffron threads, soaked in 1 pint/500 ml warm water
2 tablespoons/30 ml toasted pine nuts
1 packet bucatini pasta
Parmesan cheese, freshly grated

Cook the cauliflower in a large pan of salted, boiling water until just tender.
Drain, but keep the water for cooking the pasta. Slowly fry the onions, garlic
and currants in some of the oil until they are soft but not coloured. Add to the
pot the cauliflower, saffron with its water and the pine nuts. Continue
cooking, stirring regularly until the cauliflower has broken down to a sauce.
Keep aside until the pasta is ready.

To cook the pasta, bring the cauliflower water to the boil, add some oil and
cook until it still has a bite to it. Drain.

Meanwhile reheat the sauce, if necessary, and combine with the pasta. Serve
with the cheese.

SQUID SALAD WITH PASTA Annie Williams, artist

Ideal for a summer lunch party.

2 lb/900 g small squid (or box of frozen)
7 oz/210 g olive oil
2 teaspoons/10 ml garlic, chopped
$\frac{1}{4}$ pint/150 ml white wine
2 teaspoons/10 ml lemon juice
$\frac{1}{2}$ teaspoon/2.5 ml mustard
$\frac{1}{2}$ teaspoon/2.5 ml salt
1 tablespoon/15 ml capers

pepper to taste
1 oz/25 g fresh herbs, chopped
1 lb/450 g pasta bows
8 oz/225 g prawns, frozen or small tin
small tin of mussels (optional)
$\frac{1}{2}$ lb/225 g lightly cooked mushrooms (optional)

Prepare squid – remove head, cut off tentacles and reserve. Clean out the sac including the long flexible bone and discard. Rinse under running water, removing the layer of slime if possible. Chop into $\frac{1}{2}''$ (1 cm) slices. Heat 2 tablespoons of the oil in a pan and sauté half the garlic. Add the squid, stirring until opaque. Add the wine and a little water (3 tablespoons) and simmer covered until tender. Then uncover and cook over a brisk heat until 3 tablespoons of liquid only remain.

Mix together lemon juice, mustard, salt and the rest of the oil in a blender. Add capers, remaining garlic and season to taste.

Cook the pasta, drain and rinse under cold water. Place in serving bowl and toss with dressing. Stir in squid, etc. This dish is delicious served with a green salad and some French bread.

LASAGNETTE VENEZIANA

The Portofino and Aqualino's Bar

Serves 4 as a main course

1 lb/450 g Lasagnette pasta (can be bought at any Italian delicatessen)
14 oz/400 g tinned peeled tomatoes
14 oz/400 g broccoli spears, chopped
3 cloves garlic

Cook pasta for 10–12 minutes until *al dente*. Dry.

While pasta is cooking, prepare sauce.

Cook chopped garlic in butter until it begins to brown and then add tomatoes and broccoli and cook for half an hour.

Mix with the pasta and sprinkle lashings of Parmesan cheese over the top.

TAGLIATELLE WITH GRILLED MEDITERRANEAN VEGETABLES

Wendy Jacob, artist

1 aubergine
2 courgettes
1 green pepper
½ lb/225 g spinach
1 lb/450 g tagliatelle
butter
6 oz/175 ml single cream
salt and pepper

Wash and trim the ends off the aubergine and courgettes. Slice lengthways, then brush with oil and grill on both sides until soft.

Grill the pepper and wrap in a clean dry tea towel. Leave for a few moments then peel off the skin.

Wash the spinach, then boil in its own water until limp, stirring to prevent it burning. Drain, then squeeze out all the excess moisture.

Put the tagliatelle to cook according to the instructions on the packet.

To assemble the sauce, take the above cooked vegetables and chop together finely.

Melt some butter in a frying pan on a medium heat; add chopped vegetables and gently warm them through; add cream (take care not to let it boil), stir the mixture, check the seasoning and spoon over your tagliatelle.

Serve with some fresh grated Parmesan.

The same idea can be used with any vegetables you may have left over, although the grilled ones in the recipe taste so good that it is worth going to the trouble of making it from scratch.

opposite: Wendy Jacob

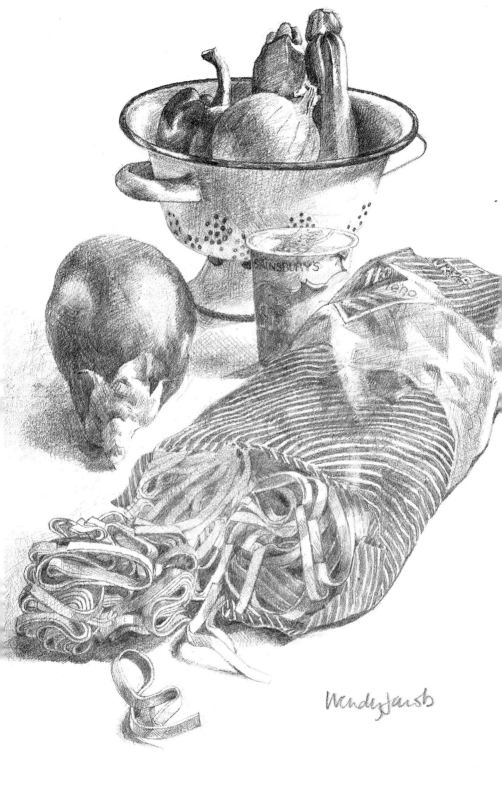

SAINSBURYS

Wendy Jacob

PASTA IN AUBERGINE SAUCE

Guido Pontecorvo, formerly Professor of Genetics

Serves 2

8 oz/200 g pasta, preferably 'Rigatoni'   1 lb/450 g aubergines, sliced
2 ½ pints/1.5 litres boiling salted water   tomato purée

Cover the aubergines with salt and leave for half an hour. Wash in cold water.

Fry the aubergines very slowly in olive oil until soft.

Mix well the pasta, which has been cooked slowly in the boiling water, aubergines and heated tomato purée. Serve and add grated Sicilian sheep cheese or Parmesan.

PASTA WITH SUN-DRIED TOMATOES

Tony Blair, MP, Sedgefield

1 lb/450 g fresh tagliatelle, fettucini or other long noodle pasta
1–2 tablespoons/15–30 ml olive oil to taste
2–3 cloves garlic
half a small bottle sun-dried tomatoes, cut into strips
2 tablespoons/30 ml chopped capers
black olives, chopped, to taste
parsley, chopped

Cook the pasta in boiling salted water with a spot of oil to prevent sticking. This takes only a few minutes for fresh pasta, about 10 minutes for dried pasta.

At the same time prepare the sauce:

Heat the olive oil in a frying pan. When hot, add the chopped garlic and cook for a few minutes to flavour the oil. Add the other ingredients to the pan and coat them all with the oil to warm through. When pasta is ready, drain and rinse with boiling water and return to the pan. Tip the contents of the frying pan into the pasta and stir so that it is coated with the sauce.

Serve with a green salad.

FERRARI'S PASTA AL CARCIOFI (GIULIAROSA'S SAUCE)

Alimentari Ferrari, delicatessen

Serves 4

1 small onion
2 cloves garlic
6 tablespoons/90 ml olive oil (virgin is a slightly stronger flavour)
$\frac{1}{2}$ jar artichoke hearts in oil and herbs
1 glass white wine
$\frac{1}{4}$ pint/150 ml single cream
1 lb/450 g pasta, any shape
6 oz/175 g freshly grated Parmesan (not packet)

Put on water for pasta.

Finely chop the onion and crush the garlic. In a large frying pan warm the olive oil and add the onion and garlic and cook on a medium heat for 2 minutes until onion is lightly golden. Add chopped artichoke hearts and cook for another 2 minutes. Add glass of white wine and continue cooking. Add cream and gently heat until cream starts to thicken. Add a small amount of the Parmesan cheese and leave on a low heat to keep warm.

Cook the pasta. When ready and drained, transfer to warm dish and add sauce and remaining Parmesan, and serve immediately.

VEGETABLE PASTA

W.G. Sinclair, Chief Superintendent, Metropolitan Police and Scotland Yard

Serves 2

6 oz/175 g pasta bows
1 carrot, peeled and sliced with potato peeler
1 courgette, sliced with potato peeler
2 tablespoons/30 ml olive oil
1 teaspoon/5 ml basil
1 teaspoon/5 ml oregano
freshly ground black pepper
Parmesan cheese

Boil pasta for about 8–10 minutes.

Meanwhile, stir fry vegetables in oil, add herbs and pepper.

Drain pasta, stir in vegetables and serve with Parmesan cheese sprinkled on top.

CORIANDER SEAFOOD CASSEROLE	56	Victor Yuan, fashion photographer
KEDGEREE	57	Nicholas Wapshott, The Times
MUSSELS	58	Robin Nicholson, architect
COPPERS' CONCOCTION	59	Rachel Callaghan, home beat officer
SUMMERHOUSE SPICY SEAFOOD SAUCE	60	Gaston Chappell, antiquarian book dealer
MEJILLONES A LA MARINERA (MUSSELS WITH WHITE WINE AND GARLIC)	60	The Finca, Tapas Bar and Restaurant
LOBSTER CREOLE	61	Renwick Carlos Lee, co-ordinator, Highbury Roundhouse Centre
CAMEMBERT AND SMOKED SALMON QUICHE	62	Sarah Knight, former cook to No. 10 Downing Street
MACKEREL AND BANANA CURRY	62	Tony Harms, At The Sign of the Chest of Drawers, pine furniture shop
SALMON FISHCAKE	63	Jeremy King, co-proprietor of The Ivy and Le Caprice
FRITO MISTO MARE	64	Dr Anthony Fry, consultant psychiatrist

FISH

SEPPIE CON NERO (CUTTLEFISH IN INK) 64 Casale Franco, restaurateur

STUFFED SQUID 66 Joe Rey, Cuba Libra Restaurant

SWEDISH MUSTARD SAUCE 66 Audrey Knight, Mange Tout, Highbury caterer

FISH STEW 67 Dr Ruth Seifert, consultant psychiatrist

STIR-FRIED SCALLOPS WITH VEGETABLES 68 Wendy Hartman, psychotherapist

COD IN ABBOT ALE BATTER 68 Philip Bulleyment, Compton Arms

KALAMARAKIA KRASSATA 69 Rena Salaman, cookery writer

KOKT TORSK MED SENAPSAS 70 Anna Hegarty, Anna's Place
(STEAMED COD WITH MUSTARD SAUCE)

FISH KEBABS WITH TOMATO CHUTNEY 71 Mr J Patel, restaurateur, Bodali

LOT AU CHAPEAU 72 Jeremy Gompertz, QC

GRAHAM'S FISH SAUCE 72 Graham Smith, 'something in the city'

THE UPPER STREET FISH SHOP RECIPE FOR HAKE 73 Olga Conway

FLAT FISH FILLETS WITH PRAWNS 74 Steve Hatt, fishmonger, Essex Road

CORIANDER SEAFOOD CASSEROLE

Victor Yuan, fashion photographer

Serves 4

1 lb/450 g uncooked king-size prawns
2 large onions
6 cloves garlic
1 dessertspoon/10 ml root ginger
5 tablespoons/75 ml olive oil
6 branches fresh coriander (dried will not do)
4 oz/125 g seafood cocktail mix
4 pieces white fish in chunks
1 small tin chopped tomatoes
2 teaspoons/10 ml tabasco
2 fl oz/60 ml single cream
2 tablespoons/30 ml tomato purée
1 lime
salt and pepper to taste

Shell prawns. Boil up shells and make a fish stock in 1 pint/500 ml water. Simmer for 25 minutes. Meanwhile peel and roughly chop onions, garlic and ginger. Place in blender with 1 tablespoon/15 ml olive oil. Add 3 pieces of coriander. Do not over blend (fine chop – not purée). Heat remaining olive oil in casserole, add blended ingredients, purée and fish stock and simmer slowly for 15 minutes until mixture becomes a rich deep red colour (important). Add all seafood, chopped tomatoes and tabasco and simmer for 5 minutes. Turn heat off, add cream and stir gently.

Serve decorated with cut limes and rest of coriander, either chopped or in branches. Serve with the following Rice and Onion dish:

1 large onion, chopped finely
vegetable oil
4 cups rice

Fry onion until very dark browny black and crispy. Cook rice, serve with onion on top.

This rice dish is a traditional Burmese dish and has an almost nutty flavour due to the burnt onions.

KEDGEREE Nicholas Wapshott, The Times

I had always thought that Kedgeree was an archetypal English dish, an essential constituent of the classic country-house breakfast, left standing on the sideboard hotplate in a covered silver bowl as a fishy alternative to the standard fare of pork sausages, tomatoes, mushrooms, eggs and fried bread. This Anglicised form, like a savoury rice pudding with lashings of butter, was how I first came to eat it.

I now know better. Kedgeree is a Persian dish and as time has gone on I have come to prefer it in the Persian style, laced with spices as the Mughal emperors enjoyed it. In recent years smart London restaurants have slipped it on the menu in a bastardised form, with salmon supplementing the smoked haddock base, and at the Ivy they tend to overdo the curry sauce. I believe it should be quite dry, with the haddock flaked and stirred among the best basmati rice, in which there should be egg, onion and traces of turmeric, cardamom and cinnamon sticks.

Serves 4

8 oz/225 g basmati rice	1 onion
4 oz/125 g butter	1 lb/450 g smoked haddock
turmeric	4 eggs
cardamom pods	salt and pepper
cinnamon stick	

Wash the rice in cold water. Take 2 oz/50 g of butter and melt in a heavy-bottomed pan. Add the spices: a teaspoon of turmeric, 3 or 4 cardamom pods, a stick of cinnamon as long as your longest finger, snapped into small pieces. Finely chop the onion and add to the mixture, increasing the temperature a little, but being careful not to brown it. Drain the rice and turn it into the spice and onion mixture. Stir and leave.

Poach the haddock in a shallow pan for 10–15 minutes. Take a pint/500 ml of the hot fish stock and stir into the rice, onion and spices. Bring to the boil, cover and simmer. After nearly 10 minutes, or when the stock is fully taken up by the rice, remove from the heat.

Boil the eggs until the white is hard and the yoke firm, but not crumbly. Slice longways and sideways. Flake and bone the smoked haddock. Fluff the spiced rice with a long-pronged fork and turn in the haddock and boiled egg. Add salt and pepper to taste. Slice the remaining butter on top and place the dish in a grill or on a fierce hotplate. Serve slightly steaming.

MUSSELS

Robin Nicholson, architect

(More a story than a recipe)

Rumours always will abound that they, over the Channel, will for ever enslave us with unnecessary regulations. Indeed, from January, even mussels from Brancaster Staithe in Norfolk will be required to be cleaned before they can be sold. But the musselers and we, their customers, know that our harbour is a rare EEC-approved OK harbour, so why do we have to do it?

Mussels are one of the most delicious cheap foods that we can get; but for those with shellfish allergies, they must be avoided and even the smell is difficult. For institutions that may be tempted by the low price of the raw ingredients, the danger is more one of over-cooking leading to chewy disappointment.

Larousse translates no less than 13 recipes, fronted by 19 centimetres of introduction to both the pleasures and the dangers, but for me there is only one on-the-spot, straight out of the marsh mussels-pit way. Along the north-west coast of Norfolk there are many proper and less proper signs from autumn to late winter advertising mussels for sale – shops, post offices and most commonly, fisherman's houses backing onto the salt marshes and their own pits.

Nearly two handfuls per person and a long session at the sink striking off the barnacles with a green scourer and pulling off their beards should leave you with a colander of clean and, if you are a perfectionist, gleaming mussels; run them under the cold water to wash off any last bits, find a large saucepan and lid and check the clock.

For each of you, chop half one (red?) onion quite finely, crush at least one clove of garlic and set aside one glass of dry white wine (each); then gently cook the onions in just enough butter – do not let them go brown. Add the garlic and wine, with some freshly chopped parsley and, if you want, a bay leaf. Just as it comes to the boil, tip in the gleaming mussels. Replace the lid, turn down the heat a bit and allow it to simmer with the occasional stir with a wooden spoon. Within minutes you will find the shells opening and when most are open remove the pan to the table or pour the contents into something less immediate first.

Serve into larger soup bowls with lots of the juice, with a large empty bowl for the empties. Neat people use one shell, like pincers, to remove the flesh and one of my partners then goes on to nest the empty shells one into the other to make a rather late punk necklace. It is most important not to force open any closed shells, which must be discarded.

Paper towels or, I suppose, steamed towels are as necessary as loads of your favourite bread, for mopping the juice, and plenty of a slightly better dry white wine. Oh, and sprinkle fresh parsley onto each bowl.

COPPERS' CONCOCTION

Rachel Callaghan, home beat officer

Makes 4–6 pancakes

Pancake:
8 oz/225 g plain flour
2 eggs
4 fl oz/100 ml milk
4 fl oz/100 ml water
pinch of salt

Filling:
1 onion, finely chopped
1 green pepper, finely chopped
4 oz/125 g prawns, cooked and peeled
4 oz/125 g mussels
Thousand Island dressing
tomato purée (to seal edges)
olive oil for frying

Fry onion and pepper for 10 minutes and set aside.

Make pancake mixture. Mix flour, eggs, milk, a little water and salt until a smooth texture is obtained.

In a pre-heated frying pan, cook pancakes on either side for approximately $1\frac{1}{2}$ minutes. Toss pancakes, if possible, or turn. Set aside.

In a separate bowl mix prawns, mussels, onion, pepper and Thousand Island dressing, to bind ingredients together.

Place quantity of filling on one side of the pancake. Use tomato purée to seal pancake edges. Fold in half. Do not overfill.

Serve HOT.

SUMMERHOUSE SPICY SEAFOOD SAUCE

Gaston Chappell, antiquarian book dealer

Serves 2, or 3 if not very hungry

olive oil	3 tinned tomatoes
few slices red pepper	3 or 4 anchovies
6 whole black peppercorns	cumin powder
cumin seeds	tabasco
1 large clove garlic	4 oz/125 g prawns
tomato paste	1 dessertspoon/10 ml thick yoghurt

Cover bottom of heavy pan with olive oil on low heat. Slice 8 thin slivers of red pepper. When oil is hot, add the red pepper, followed by peppercorns. Stir. Add a good pinch of cumin seeds and fry all this gently. Add garlic, cut into pieces, then a good squeeze of tomato paste. After a minute or so, add 3 tinned tomatoes and the anchovies, sliced small. Add pinch of cumin powder and about 4 shakes of tabasco. Simmer for 5 minutes, then throw in the prawns and thicken with yoghurt, but beware of curdling.

Serve with pasta, preferably linguine.

MEJILLONES A LA MARINERA
(Mussels with White Wine and Garlic)

The Finca, Tapas Bar and Restaurant

Serves 4

You will need a large pan with a lid.

2 lb/900 g cleaned mussels in the shell	½ cup white wine
½ onion, finely diced	salt and pepper
1 clove garlic, chopped	3 tablespoons/45 ml olive oil

Heat the oil in pan, add onions and garlic and fry for a few minutes. Add the mussels, wine, salt and pepper. Cover with lid and cook for 10–15 minutes on a low heat until all mussels are opened – discard any that stay closed.

Serve with mixed salad and lots of bread, the sauce from this is yummy.

LOBSTER CREOLE

Renwick Carlos Lee, co-ordinator, Highbury Roundhouse Centre

This is a traditional family recipe from Jamaica and reflects the influences of both the Caribbean and Latin America.

Serves 6

2 cups red peas (kidney beans)
1 large bacon knuckle
$\frac{1}{2}$ lb/225 g small chicken pieces, with bone
2 cloves garlic, crushed
2 stalks escallion, crushed
2 large peppers, one green, one red
black pepper

1 whole hot pepper
1 sprig thyme
2 bay leaves
1 pre-cooked lobster
6 large prawns
2 fl oz/60 ml coconut cream

The red peas, if fresh, will need soaking overnight. Soak the bacon knuckle in plenty of water for an hour.

Throw the water away from both the peas and the knuckle and place them in a large pan. Cover with water and bring to the boil. Simmer for at least 2 hours until the peas are very soft and almost disintegrating. Add water, if needed, during cooking.

Meanwhile, brown the chicken pieces in a little oil, adding the garlic, escallion (or onions), the green and red peppers, black pepper and the whole hot pepper, plus the herbs. Add to the other ingredients and cook down slowly.

To prepare the lobster, cut it in half lengthways and clean, then cut into sections with the shell. The prawns should be used whole with shells. Add to the other ingredients and cook through thoroughly but gently.

Finally, add the coconut cream, stirring in gently until fully dissolved and cooked.

To thicken, if needed, mash in some of the peas on the side of the pan.

Serve piping hot with white fluffy rice, fried sliced plantains, avocado slices and salad.

CAMEMBERT AND SMOKED SALMON QUICHE

Sarah Knight, former cook to No. 10 Downing Street

6 sheets filo pastry
2 oz/50 g butter, melted
7 oz/200 g Camembert cheese
4 eggs
4 oz/125 g smoked salmon
¾ pint/375 ml single cream or milk and cream mixed
1 tablespoon/15 ml dill, chopped
seasoning to taste

Line a greased 10″(25 cm) quiche dish or flan tin with one sheet of the pastry, brush with butter, top with another sheet of pastry, brush with butter. Arrange the sheets of pastry so they evenly cover the dish. Continue layering and buttering until all the pastry is used. Trim edges with scissors. Remove rind from Camembert, slice the cheese thinly and place evenly in the pastry case. Blend or process eggs, salmon, cream, dill and seasoning together. Pour into pastry case. Bake in a moderate oven, 350F/180C/gas mark 4, for about 40 minutes or until set.

A little grated cheddar cheese, sprinkled on the top of the quiche before baking, can be added.

Smoked salmon trimmings are ideal for this recipe.

MACKEREL AND BANANA CURRY

Tony Harms, At The Sign of the Chest of Drawers, pine furniture shop

Cut a medium-sized banana into 1″(2.5 cm) long pieces and soak in water for 2 hours or longer. In a frying pan melt 2 oz/50 g cooking butter. Blend 1 chilli, half an onion, 1″(2.5 cm) ginger root and a clove of garlic and fry on a low heat for 5 minutes. Add ½ teaspoon/2.5 ml of cumin powder and the same of turmeric. After 2 minutes add the banana and cook slowly for 10 minutes. Add 1 tablespoon/25 ml desiccated coconut and 1 of breadcrumbs and cook for a further 5 minutes. Stuff a large mackerel with the mixture and microwave, using the times given in your guide book.

SALMON FISHCAKE

Jeremy King, co-proprietor of The Ivy and Le Caprice

An original Caprice dish:

Makes 8 fishcakes

$1\frac{1}{2}$ lb/675 g salmon fillet, clean of any bone and skin, poached
$1\frac{1}{2}$ lb/675 g plain, dry mashed potato
2 tablespoons/30 ml tomato ketchup
1 tablespoon/15 ml English mustard
1 tablespoon/15 ml anchovy essence
salt and pepper to taste

For the sauce:
1 pint/500 ml strong fish stock
2/3rds glass dry white wine
$1\frac{1}{2}$ oz/40 g butter
1 oz/25 g plain flour
2 oz/50 g fresh sorrel
$\frac{1}{2}$ pint/300 ml double cream
salt and pepper to taste

To make the fishcake:
In a mixing bowl with a spoon mix the potato, half the quantity of poached salmon, ketchup, anchovy and mustard and seasoning until a smooth paste. Flake in the remaining salmon and fold in gently. Season the mixture and mould into round cakes (about $2\frac{1}{2}''$ (6 cm) diameter × $1\frac{3}{4}''$ (4.5 cm) deep). Refrigerate.

To make the sauce:
Bring the fish stock to the boil in a thick bottomed pan. In another pan melt the butter and stir in the flour. Cook very slowly over a low heat for 30 seconds. Whisk the flour mixture into the fish stock. Add the white wine and simmer for 30 minutes until thickened. Shred the sorrel and add to the sauce with the double cream. Season to taste.

To serve:
Lightly flour the fishcakes and pan fry, colouring each side. Cook in the oven for 10 minutes at 400F/200C/gas mark 6. Serve on a bed of spinach with the sauce over the fishcake.

FRITO MISTO MARE

Dr Anthony Fry, consultant psychiatrist

Frito Misto Mare is, of course, a firm Italian favourite and a dish which can be surprisingly easy to cook with the increasingly exotic fish carried by local fishmongers and market stalls. A simple version uses prawns and squid.

Peel the prawns and let them dry out thoroughly. Cut and gut the squid, washing out all the ink in a sink full of warm water. Then cut into round pieces and drop the round washed pieces into boiling water to blanch them. Do not boil them. Remove immediately from the boiling water and dry them on a clean cloth or some tissue. When they are quite dry, roll them in flour and drop them and the prawns into a deep fryer full of olive oil. Cook until they are just golden brown, remove from the deep fryer and drain on a wire rack. Serve hot with large pieces of lemon and black pepper.

Many people enjoy a little garlic with this dish, but be very careful not to fry the garlic as this spoils the taste. Sliced garlic cloves should be dropped into the oil very briefly until they begin to turn very slightly golden brown. They should then be removed and mixed in with the fish.

Serve with a chilled dry Corvo followed with a large green salad with a sharp dressing made with red wine vinegar, olive oil and a touch of mustard.

SEPPIE CON NERO (Cuttlefish in Ink)

Casale Franco Pizzeria Ristorante

Serves 4

2 lb/1 kg small cuttlefish with ink
olive oil
1 onion, sliced
1 clove garlic, chopped

1 glass dry white wine
1 small tin tomato purée
salt and pepper

Carefully clean the cuttlefish, removing the beak and detaching the ink sac without piercing it. Put the ink sacs aside. In a pan heat a little olive oil and sweat the onion and garlic for a few minutes until soft. Add the cuttlefish and toss for a minute, then add the wine. Bring up to the boil, then add enough water to cover the fish. Continue to boil for a few minutes then add tomato purée and seasoning.

Pour a little warm water into the bowl containing the ink sacs. Break each sac with the point of a knife and pass this mixture of ink and water through a colander into another bowl.

When most of the liquid has evaporated from the cuttlefish, add the ink mixture. Reduce the heat and simmer gently for about $1\frac{1}{2}$ hours, until the sauce has thickened and the cuttlefish is tender.

At Casale Franco we serve our Seppie Con Nero with grilled polenta as a main course, or with spaghetti as a starter.

Juliet Lawson

STUFFED SQUID Joe Rey, Cuba Libra Restaurant

Serves 10

2 onions, well chopped
2 teaspoons/10 ml garlic purée
2 teaspoons/10 ml fish stock
1 dessertspoon/10 ml parsley, chopped
4 oz/125 g cornmeal
2 green peppers, chopped small
4 bay leaves
4 fl oz/100 ml dry white wine
2 teaspoons/10 ml cracked black pepper
2 teaspoons/10 ml salt
2 lb/900 g squid, cleaned and cartilage and bone removed
5 red peppers, chopped small
10 medium-sized squid (for stuffing)
7 oz/200 g tomato sauce, homemade if possible

Place all the ingredients in a saucepan, except the 10 medium-sized squid, red peppers and tomato sauce. Leave the ingredients to cook for 30 minutes at medium heat. Then place mixture in the blender.

Clean the squid and fill each with the mixture from the blender and close with a cocktail stick. Cover each in flour and fry in cooking oil until slightly brown. Place on a dish, top with the chopped peppers and tomato sauce, and cover with foil and cook in oven at 375F/190C/gas mark 5 for an hour. Remove the cocktail sticks before serving. Serve with a small salad.

SWEDISH MUSTARD SAUCE

Audrey Knight, Mange Tout, Highbury caterer

This has got to be one of the most delicious sauces for smoked salmon, smoked halibut, gravadlax, salmon pasties or home-cooked ham.

7 tablespoons/100 ml oil
2 tablespoons/30 ml wine vinegar
1½ tablespoons/20 ml brown sugar

salt and pepper

2 dessertspoons/20 ml Dijon or Grainy mustard

2 egg yolks

2 tablespoons/30 ml fresh dill, chopped

Mix all ingredients in a food processor. It makes a thick mayonnaise-like sauce. You can, of course, adjust the amounts according to taste.

FISH STEW

Dr Ruth Seifert, consultant psychiatrist

1 onion, chopped	$1\frac{1}{2}$ lb/675 g squid
2 cloves garlic, crushed	$\frac{1}{2}$ green chilli
1 bay leaf	2 large tomatoes, skinned and chopped
1 red pepper, chopped	salt and pepper to taste
$1\frac{1}{2}$ lb/675 g mussels	handful fresh basil, shredded
1 glass white wine	double cream, small carton
$1\frac{1}{2}$ lb/675 g monkfish	

Cook mussels: fry $\frac{1}{4}$ onion, 1 clove of garlic, bay leaf and $\frac{1}{2}$ red pepper. Fry 1–2 minutes over high heat and add the washed mussels in their shells. When open, put in glass of white wine and turn off the heat. Leave covered.

Cook monkfish and squid: in a wide shallow pan fry $\frac{1}{2}$ onion, 1 clove of garlic, $\frac{1}{2}$ red pepper, $\frac{1}{2}$ green chilli. Fry for 1–2 minutes until soft, then add the monkfish cut into $1\frac{1}{2}''$ (4 cm) cubes. Cook for 5 minutes and then add the squid. Cook for a few minutes and then add the skinned and chopped tomatoes with a good splash of white wine. Add salt and pepper to taste and basil leaves and cook uncovered to reduce the liquid by half.

Finally strain the mussels and reduce the strained liquid by half. Remove mussels from shells and discard shells. Add the mussels and their reduced liquid to the monkfish and squid stew and heat for a minute. Place in a shallow serving dish and keep warm. Just before serving, add the cream.

Serve hot with crusty French bread.

STIR-FRIED SCALLOPS WITH VEGETABLES

Wendy Hartman, psychotherapist

Serves 2

This recipe arose out of my need to concoct something which allowed for all family culinary idiosyncracies – ie. veggie, and wheat, eggs, and dairy-free. If you are feeling poor you can substitute skate knobs (from the fish stall in Chapel Street market) – they are a bit more work and require careful trimming but the flesh is firm and sweet. Otherwise, go for broke and buy scallops – 2 per person.

2 plump cloves of garlic	2 spring onions
1″ (2.5 cm) fresh ginger	ground coriander
1 chilli pepper	slivers of orange rind
1 large carrot	nam pla
1 large courgette	soy sauce
8 oz/225 g skate knobs, or 4 scallops	tamarind or lemon juice

Stir-fry finely chopped garlic, ginger and chilli in a little oil for a minute, add matchsticks of carrot and courgette for a further minute or so, followed by sliced scallops, or chunks of skate knobs, and chopped spring onions. Stir around for a moment or two and slosh in a dessertspoon/10 ml of nam pla and some soy sauce, 1 teaspoon/5 ml ground coriander, 1 dessertspoon/10 ml of blanched, slivered orange rind and some tamarind or lemon juice. Cook, stirring continuously for a further couple of minutes or until just cooked to your taste, with a bit of a bite to the vegetables.

Serve with Chinese rice noodles.

COD IN ABBOT ALE BATTER

Philip Bulleyment, The Compton Arms

To cover 4 × 6–7 oz/175–200 g fillets of cod you will need:

12 tablespoons/180 ml plain flour

1 teaspoon/5 ml of bicarbonate of soda
1 tablespoon/15 ml vinegar (to brown the batter)
1 × 15 fl oz/440 ml can of Greene King Abbot ale

Cover your fish in plain flour, then dip into the batter mix (which you have whisked into a pancake texture). Cook in deep oil, hot, till golden brown.

Serve with home-made chips and mushy peas.

KALAMARAKIA KRASSATA

Rena Salaman, cookery writer

Serves 4–6

A delicious and easy way of cooking squid. It can be served with pasta as a main meal, or with rice, or on its own as a first course with crusty bread for the delicious sauce. Any size squid can be used, though medium-sized are best for this recipe. Very large squid will need to be cooked a little longer.

2 lbs/1 kg squid	$\frac{1}{2}$ teaspoon/2.5 ml marjoram
5 tablespoons/75 ml olive oil	salt and black pepper
1 lb/450 g onions, sliced	2 small tomatoes, chopped
1 glass dry white wine	1 sweet red pepper, de-seeded
$\frac{1}{4}$ pint/150 ml water	and cut into thin strips

Prepare the squid by pulling the heads from the bodies. Slit each body open and empty it of all its innards. Pull the two little flaps away and peel off the film which covers the body. Rinse everything carefully and strain. Cut the upper part of the head underneath the eyes, being careful not to splash yourself with the ink, and discard. Rinse tentacles. Slice the bodies in 1″(2.5 cm) wide strips.

Sauté the onions in the hot oil, add the squid and fry fiercely, stirring, until all the liquid has evaporated and it starts to stick. Pour in the wine and then the water, herbs and seasoning. Cover and cook gently for 20 minutes, stirring occasionally to prevent sticking. Add the tomatoes and pepper and cook for a further 5–10 minutes. The sauce should be substantially thick, made deliciously sweet by the melted onions.

KOKT TORSK MED SENAPSAS
(Steamed Cod with Mustard Sauce)

Anna Hegarty, Anna's Place

2 lbs/1 kg fresh North Atlantic cod
2 tablespoons/30 ml lemon juice
salt
1½ pints/750 ml water
1 bay leaf
bunch of dill or parsley stalks
4 peppercorns
1 leek, chopped
1 carrot, chopped

The sauce:
2 oz/50 g butter
¾ oz/20 g flour
½ pint/250 ml fish stock
½ pint/250 ml fresh cream
2–3 tablespoons/30–45 ml mustard seeds, crushed
pepper and salt
pinch of sugar

Sprinkle the cleaned cod with lemon juice, season with salt and cut each fish into 4 steaks. Bring water to the boil with the bay leaf, stalks, peppercorns and the chopped carrot and leek. Reduce the heat, and add the cod slices. Leave for 10–12 minutes to simmer according to the size of the cod – but do not allow to boil. Remove cod carefully with a slotted spoon and keep warm.

To make the sauce:

Melt butter and stir in the flour to make a roux. Stir in the fish stock slowly, add cream and allow to cook gently. Season with salt, pepper, crushed mustard seeds and a little sugar to taste.

Arrange the fish on a large dish with dill or parsley and lemon wedges. Serve the sauce separately, with fresh boiled potatoes and buttered green peas to go with the fish.

FISH KEBABS WITH TOMATO CHUTNEY

Mr J. Patel restaurateur, Bodali

Serves 8

2 green chillies (3 if you like it hot)
¼ bunch fresh coriander
2–3 cloves garlic (4 if you like garlic)
1 large onion
1½ lb/675 g cod
salt to taste
3 teaspoons/15 ml cumin powder

4 oz/125 g ground cloves
4 oz/125 g ground cinnamon
3 eggs
4 oz/125 g breadcrumbs
6–8 dessertspoons/60–80 ml good
    vegetable oil
black pepper, optional

Liquidise green chillies, coriander, garlic and onion with as little water as possible. Boil the cod with salted water to cover for about 4–6 minutes. Remove and place in bowl with the liquidised ingredients; add the dry spices, beaten eggs and breadcrumbs and mash together with a fork. Pour the oil in a frying pan and heat over a medium heat. Wet your left hand with water, take a fistful of the mixture with that hand, make it into a flattened ball (like a burger). Fry these 'burgers' very slowly and gently in the heated oil. When brown on both sides, dry on kitchen towel to remove the oil. Serve with Tomato Chutney.

Tomato Chutney:

1 large Spanish onion
2 green chillies
3–4 cloves garlic
1 large tin good quality tomatoes

salt and sugar, to taste
1½ teaspoon/7.5 ml cumin powder
4 dessertspoons/40 ml desiccated coconut

Liquidise the onion, chillies and garlic with the liquid from the tin of tomatoes. Remove from liquidiser and liquidise the tomatoes. Mix the two in a bowl and add salt and sugar to taste, plus the cumin and coconut. Leave in fridge overnight as it improves the flavour.

Keeps in a jar in the fridge for a week.

The skin on frozen fish will peel off under tap water.

For breadcrumbs you can use toast crushed in a coffee grinder.

LOT AU CHAPEAU Jeremy Gompertz, QC

A really simple recipe for the idle and incompetent bachelor.

Serves 4

2 ½ lbs/1.15 kg monkfish (gross weight)
3 lemons
1 teaspoon/5 ml olive oil
3–4 cloves garlic, crushed

a little oregano
butter for frying
½ cup dry white wine
2 tablespoons/30 ml cream

Skin, fillet and dice the fish (1″/2.5 cm).

Marinate the fish for 5–6 hours in mixture of lemon juice, olive oil, 2–3 crushed cloves of garlic and a sprinkle of oregano.

Lightly sauté the fish in the butter and wine for 6–8 minutes adding a little more crushed garlic and oregano. Thicken the marinade and stir in the cream for a sauce.

Serve with plain boiled rice or potatoes.

No marks for guessing why this recipe is so named.

GRAHAM'S FISH SAUCE

Graham Smith, 'something in the city'

Enough for 4

1 tablespoon/15 ml olive oil
½ teaspoon/2.5 ml cumin
½ teaspoon/2.5 ml mustard seeds
1 clove garlic
1 medium onion, chopped
tin of chopped tomatoes

pinch of tarragon
¼ teaspoon/1.25 ml dried
   Mediterranean herbs
pinch of cayenne pepper
½ teaspoon/2.5 ml garam masala
1 tablespoon/15 ml plain yoghurt

Put olive oil in saucepan, add cumin and mustard seeds, then add garlic and onion. Once onion is clear add tomatoes, tarragon, herbs and cayenne pepper. Simmer for 4–5 minutes, and when ready remove from heat and add garam masala and yoghurt. Pour over any white fish. Put in oven until fish is cooked.

THE UPPER STREET FISH SHOP RECIPE FOR HAKE

Olga Conway, The Upper Street Fish Shop

Serves 4

2 teaspoons/10 ml olive oil
1 medium onion, chopped
2 oz/50 g mushrooms, chopped
8 oz/225 g tomatoes, skinned and chopped
2 cloves garlic, crushed
$\frac{1}{2}$ teaspoon/2.5 ml tomato purée
$\frac{1}{2}$ glass white wine
$\frac{1}{2}$ teaspoon/2.5 ml mixed herbs
salt and pepper to taste
4 pieces of hake; fillets or cutlets
1 lemon

Heat olive oil in frying pan, add onions and sweat gently for 5–10 minutes until soft. Add all the other ingredients, except the fish and the juice of 1 lemon. Bring to the boil and simmer for 20–30 minutes until most of the moisture has gone.

Meanwhile heat the grill to the highest setting. When very hot, place the pieces of hake under the grill seasoned with lemon juice, olive oil, salt and pepper. Grill for 10–15 minutes, turning once. When almost cooked, spread the tomato mixture over each piece and return to the grill for 2 minutes.

Serve with new potatoes and salad.

FLAT FISH FILLETS WITH PRAWNS

Steve Hatt, fishmonger, Essex Road

Chosen by Steve Hatt for George Graham, Manager of the Arsenal Football Team, winners of the Coca Cola Cup and the F.A. Cup 1993, a first in football history.

Serves 2

Take either:

	1 Dover sole large enough for 2 people (ie $1\frac{1}{4}$–$1\frac{3}{4}$lb/550g–800g)
or	2 × 8 oz/225 g plaice fillets
or	1 large or 2 small lemon soles

Larger size fish are preferable as they should be filleted into quarters. Roll the skinned fillets horizontally giving a vol au vent effect, and stuff the centre of each with 5 or 6 peeled prawns. Place the fillets on a baking tray or oven-to-table serving dish. Cover with foil and cook for 7–9 minutes at preheated temperature, 350F/180C/gas mark 4.

These look very pretty with the pink centre in the white meat. Can be eaten with just a fork and are fast to produce. Lovely topped with a standard Hollandaise sauce.

SUPREMES OF CHICKEN WITH ASPARAGUS	78	Nicolas Huntington, Moveable Feasts
SAGE CHICKEN	78	Rupert Perry, Islington Councillor and finalist in 1988 Observer cookery competition
COLD CHICKEN PIE	79	Judith Cox, NSPCC Committee
LAZY CHICKEN CASSEROLE	80	Robert McCrum, publisher and writer
HOT CHICKEN SALAD	80	Susan Bradshaw, concert pianist
CHICKEN IN MANGO AND GINGER SAUCE	81	Audrey Knight, Mange Tout, Highbury caterer
HERBED CHICKEN EGUSI SOUP	82	Sade, singer
SPICY COCONUT CHICKEN	82	Angela Neustatter, journalist and writer
MAIZE-FED CHICKEN WITH GARLIC AND LEMON SAUCE	84	Stephen Bull, restaurateur
BANG BANG CHICKEN	84	Charles Fontaine, The Quality Chop House

CHICKEN & GAME

POULET BLEU	86	Jill Tweedie, writer and journalist
BAKED LEMON CHICKEN	86	Jenny Blanchard, designer
CHICKEN WITH FRUIT	87	Diana Huntley, antique dealer, Camden Passage
PLUM DUCK	88	Andrew Mitchell, MP, Gedling
DUCK SALAD	88	Emma Hope, shoe designer
CORONATION CHICKEN	89	Annette Ludvigsen, NSPCC Committee
GLOUCESTERSHIRE PHEASANT	90	Sally Beauman, novelist
PARTRIDGE IN A POT	91	Rodney Slatford, musician
SLOW COOKED GUINEA FOWL WITH POLENTA	92	Justin Cartwright, novelist
PIGEONS EN COCOTTE	93	David Simon, Chief Executive & Deputy Chairman BP
RABBIT CASSEROLE	94	John Murray Brown, Angel Bookshop

SUPREMES OF CHICKEN WITH ASPARAGUS

Nicolas Huntington, Moveable Feasts

Serves 6

6 boned and skinned chicken supremes
2 oz/50 g butter
1 glass dry white vermouth (Noilly Prat)
1 tin asparagus cuts

1 oz/25 g flour
½ pint/250 ml milk
6 oz/175 g whipping cream

Place the chicken supremes in a baking dish with 1 oz/25 g butter, the vermouth and juice from the tinned asparagus. Cover and poach in a moderate oven, 350F/180C/gas mark 4, for 30 minutes.

Make a white sauce using 1 oz/25 g flour, 1 oz/25 g butter and ½ pint/250 ml milk. Add to this the juices from the poached chicken. Liquidise the asparagus cuts and add to the sauce. Bring the sauce to the boil ensuring the flour is cooked; then add the cream. Cover the chicken with the sauce and reheat. Serve with new potatoes and baby carrots.

SAGE CHICKEN

Rupert Perry, Islington Councillor and finalist in the 1988 Observer Cookery Competition.

Serves 6

1 medium chicken
6 medium potatoes

3 cloves garlic
1 bunch sage

olive oil

Heat oven to 400F/200C/gas mark 6. Cut chicken along the breast and lay flat, skin down, on rack over roasting pan with potatoes, quartered, peeled or unpeeled, around edges of the pan.

Press chopped garlic and sage leaves on chicken, pour on some olive oil and place in oven for 25 minutes. After 25 minutes turn chicken, skin side up. Baste potatoes and sprinkle some salt on the skin, cook for a further 25 minutes.

Serve with a green salad.

COLD CHICKEN PIE Judith Cox, NSPCC Committee

Adapted from a Delia Smith recipe

This is a delicious pie, which freezes well, very suitable for picnics or outdoor lunches.

Pastry:
2 oz/50 g lard at room temperature
2 oz/50 g butter at room temperature

8 oz/225 g flour, sifted
cold water
beaten egg to glaze

Filling:
4 chicken breasts, skinned
1 teaspoon/5 ml mace, powdered
salt and freshly milled black pepper
1 lb/450 g pork sausagemeat
4 spring onions, finely chopped
1 teaspoon/5 ml fresh thyme, or $\frac{1}{2}$ teaspoon/2.5 ml dried
1 tablespoon/15 ml fresh sage, chopped, or $\frac{1}{2}$ teaspoon/2.5 ml dried
rind and juice of half a lemon
2 tablespoons/30 ml double cream

Pre-heat oven to 400F/200C/gas mark 6.

Make the pastry by rubbing the fats into the sifted flour until the mixture resembles fine breadcrumbs, then add just enough water so the dough leaves the bowl clean. Rest the dough in a polythene bag in the fridge for half an hour, then use half to line a round 8″(20 cm) diameter × 2″(5 cm) deep pie dish.

Next, cut the chicken into $\frac{1}{2}$″(1.25 cm) pieces, place them in a bowl, add the mace and season with salt and pepper. In a separate bowl combine the sausagemeat with spring onions, thyme and sage, the lemon rind and two spoons of lemon juice. Pour the cream and mix everything together well to make a soft mixture (rather like a cake mix) – if necessary, add a little more cream. Put one-third of the sausagemeat mixture in the bottom of the pastry-lined tin and spread it flat. Put half the chicken pieces on top and sprinkle in the remaining lemon juice, then add another layer of one-third sausagemeat, followed by the rest of the chicken and a final layer of sausagemeat.

Roll out the rest of the pastry and use it to cover the pie – which will be well piled up, dome-like, by now. Seal the edges well, glaze with some beaten egg and bake on a baking sheet in the pre-heated oven for 30 minutes. Then reduce the heat to 350F/180C/gas mark 4 and cook for a further $1\frac{1}{4}$ hours.

LAZY CHICKEN CASSEROLE

Robert McCrum, publisher and writer

Serves 6

1–2 large onions	3 cans Campbells condensed
6 chicken breasts, skinned and cubed	mushroom soup
6 handfuls small button mushrooms	1–2 cups fresh Parmesan cheese, grated
1 large packet frozen broccoli	approximately $\frac{1}{4}$ bottle white wine

Chop the onion and sauté in 3–4 tablespoons/45–60 ml olive oil until translucent. Transfer to a large casserole dish. Then sauté the chicken pieces, adding more oil to the pan if necessary, and add to the onion when cooked. Next sauté the mushrooms in the remaining oil, adding to the onion and chicken when done. Lastly, add the packet of frozen broccoli. Meanwhile, mix the soup with the Parmesan and wine, then pour over the chicken and vegetables, mixing thoroughly. Place in the oven and cook, covered, for approximately 1 hour at 400F/200C/gas mark 6.

HOT CHICKEN SALAD

Susan Bradshaw, concert pianist

This recipe, which I've enjoyed over the years, comes from an international collection that was published in 1957 and sold to raise money for the United Nations Nursery School in Geneva. This is one of the American contributions – hence the cup measurements (see conversion table).

2 cups chicken or turkey, diced	2 tablespoons/30 ml lemon juice
$\frac{1}{4}$ cup chicken stock	2 tablespoons/30 ml onion, grated
1$\frac{1}{2}$ cups celery, diced	salt and pepper
1 cup salted almonds, chopped	$\frac{3}{4}$ cup potato crisps, crushed
1 pimento, chopped	$\frac{1}{2}$ cup cheese, grated
1 cup mayonnaise	6 grapefruit shells

Heat chicken in stock over a low heat, stirring occasionally until thoroughly warmed. Remove pan from stove and add celery, nuts, pimento and mayonnaise (blended with lemon juice and onion); mix well, add seasoning to taste. Pile in shells, sprinkle crisps and cheese over each serving, then bake in oven at 425F/220C/gas mark 7 for about 10 minutes.

CHICKEN IN MANGO AND GINGER SAUCE

Audrey Knight, Mange Tout, Highbury caterer

Serves 4

3 oz/75 g butter
2 mangoes
1½ teaspoons/7.5 ml fresh ginger, finely chopped
1 bunch of fresh coriander, chopped
cream
salt and pepper
4 chicken breasts, skinned
chicken stock, preferably homemade

Melt the butter in a pan, add the chopped flesh of 1½ mangoes and the chopped ginger. Cook for a few minutes over moderate heat. Process the mixture until smooth, add the chopped coriander (saving a few sprigs for decoration) and process again briefly and thin the sauce with a little cream. Add salt and pepper to taste. In the meantime poach the chicken in the stock. When the chicken is cooked, place on a serving dish, pour the sauce over and decorate with the remaining half mango cut into slices and the sprigs of fresh coriander.

This is a delicious, quick and healthy main course served with some new potatoes and a green salad.

I make this dish for vast numbers of people and I add the ginger and coriander according to taste. It is always very popular.

HERBED CHICKEN EGUSI SOUP

Sade, singer

This is a juicy dish from my country, Nigeria – this is my way of making it.

1 medium chicken
salt to taste
½ medium tomato
1 small onion
1 small fresh chilli pepper
3 fl oz/70 ml palm oil
10 oz/275 g ground egusi seeds*, (roasted or unroasted melon seeds)
½ lb/225 g tea bush leaves* or spinach, (frozen is fine)

Cut the chicken into small pieces, breaking the large bones. Cover with water, adding the salt and boil (covered) on a low heat until tender and the liquid is reduced to three quarters of its original volume. Skim off any oil from the surface.

Pulp the tomato, onion and chilli pepper and fry gently in the palm oil for 2 minutes. Add the ground egusi and fry for a further 2 minutes. Now add these ingredients and the tea bush leaves to the chicken and broth and simmer uncovered for 20 minutes.

Serve with eba*, fufu*, pounded yam*, tuwo* or rice.

* these ingredients can be found at most Afro-Caribbean food suppliers.

SPICY COCONUT CHICKEN

Angela Neustatter, journalist and writer

Serves 6

This is a recipe created on the hoof for a dinner party. It had to be created at top speed as I got a sudden commission for an article which took up most of the time I had allotted for leisurely cooking. As sometimes happens with the haphazard, it was greeted as a great success and since then I have formalised the recipe and used it many times.

2 medium onions

enough oil to cover the bottom of the largest size frying pan

$\frac{1}{2}$ lb/225 g small mushrooms

2 oz/50 g sultanas

2 cloves garlic

nob of skinned fresh ginger

1 dessertspoon/10 ml cardamom pods

1 dessertspoon/10 ml caraway seed

1 dessertspoon/10 ml fenugreek

1 dessertspoon/10 ml poppy seed

4 oz/125 g desiccated coconut

2 oz/50 g creamed coconut

$\frac{1}{2}$ pint/250 ml water with 2 chicken bouillon cubes dissolved in it

1 tablespoon/15 ml brown sugar

salt to taste

6 large chicken portions, skinned

Fry the onion in the oil and add chopped mushrooms, sultanas, chopped garlic and chopped ginger and fry for 2 minutes.

Meanwhile put cardamom pods, caraway seed, fenugreek, poppy seed and ginger into a grinder and grind as finely as possible. Add this to the frying pan along with the desiccated coconut and creamed coconut and cook everything for 1 minute. Add the bouillon dissolved in water, the brown sugar and 1 teaspoon/5 ml of salt and mix all together.

Place the chicken portions in an ovenproof dish and pour the frying pan mixture over the top. Cover with silver foil. Put into an oven at 350F/180C/ gas mark 4 and cook for 30 minutes. Take out of the oven, remove foil, then cook for another 15 minutes.

Meanwhile cook enough pilao rice for 6 people, timed to have ready with the chicken dish. Serve with a green salad.

MAIZE-FED CHICKEN WITH GARLIC AND LEMON SAUCE

Stephen Bull, restaurateur

Serves 6

$\frac{1}{4}$ oz/6 g butter
1 oz/25 g shallots, finely chopped
sprig of thyme
4 cloves of garlic, crushed with salt
1 bay leaf
zest and juice of 1 lemon
approx. 1 teaspoon/5 ml sugar
$\frac{1}{4}$ pint/150 ml chicken stock made from chicken bones
$\frac{1}{4}$ pint/150 ml white wine
$\frac{1}{2}$ pint/250 ml double cream
salt and freshly ground black pepper
1 oz/25 g parsley or tarragon, chopped
2 maize-fed chickens, jointed as for sauté (bones reserved for stock)

Sweat shallots in butter until translucent, add thyme, garlic and bay leaf.

Add lemon juice, sugar, chicken stock, white wine and cream and reduce until coating consistency is reached.

Pass through a fine sieve, season with salt and pepper to taste, add zest of lemon and chopped herbs and use immediately with the sauted chicken pieces, and Celeriac and Potato Gratin Dauphinois (see p.57).

BANG BANG CHICKEN

Charles Fontaine, The Quality Chop House

Serves 4 main courses or 6 starters

This dish was originally from Thailand and is served in a lot of London restaurants.

There is quite a lot of preparation involved, but no cooking time, which makes it perfect to serve as a starter or light lunch.

1 large cucumber
6 leaves round lettuce
6 leaves radicchio
4 spring onions
1 lb/450 g smoked chicken, clean of skin and bone (breast is preferable)
4 limes
10 tablespoons/150 ml smooth peanut butter
10 tablespoons/150 ml good virgin olive oil
1 tablespoon/15 ml sweet chilli sauce
salt and pepper

Peel and remove the seeds from the cucumber. Cut into 4 chunks, slice into match-size sticks and keep to one side in a small bowl.

Clean and roll lettuce and cut into shreds. Put aside as with cucumber.

Clean and finely shred the spring onions and again place in a bowl.

Take chicken meat and clean off any bones and skin. Cut into long thin pieces.

The cucumber, lettuce, onions and chicken should all be consistent in size. Place all four bowls in the fridge to keep them fresh.

Squeeze 3 limes into a mixing bowl, add the peanut butter, 8 tablespoons/120 ml olive oil and the chilli sauce. To test the texture of the sauce you should plunge a spoon into the mixture. The spoon should be coated on both sides, rather like melted chocolate. If it is too thick, add a little water. Season to taste.

In a different bowl squeeze the remaining lime and add the rest of the olive oil. Mix and season to taste.

Take 6 cold medium-sized plates and place the cucumber, onions, lettuce and chicken in 4 separate heaps on each plate. Coat the chicken with the peanut sauce and sprinkle the vegetables with the lime and olive dressing, then serve.

POULET BLEU

Jill Tweedie, journalist and writer

1 or 2 onions, chopped	milk
butter	decent slice blue cheese
1 chicken, dismembered	parsley
salt and pepper	

Use a suitably sized and nice-looking hob-to-table casserole. Simmer onions in butter until soft. Add salted and peppered chicken pieces and fry until they take on an appetising colour. Then pour in enough milk to cover and crumble in the blue cheese – the cheapest works perfectly well. Simmer the whole, uncovered, until the chicken is done.

Serve with tagliatelle or egg noodles. The great thing about this dish is, it is easy, takes very little preparation time and has a deliciously unusual taste. Oh, I forgot, sprinkle the chopped parsley on 5 minutes before serving.

BAKED LEMON CHICKEN

Jenny Blanchard, designer

The source of this recipe is Jocasta Innes.

The essence of this Greek dish is simplicity and flexibility – you could substitute slices or chops of pork or lamb – and a good tempered way of being able to take longer cooking without falling to bits. Lots of freshly squeezed lemon juice is the flavouring secret.

Serves 8–10

2 × 3–3½ lb/1.5 kg chickens, jointed
salt and black pepper
4 tablespoons/60 ml flour
oil for frying
2 lbs/900 g potatoes, peeled and thickly sliced
6 cloves garlic, peeled and chopped
2 tablespoons/30 ml fresh herbs, chopped, such as tarragon, oregano, thyme
    or parsley, or 1 teaspoon/5 ml dried herbs
¾ pint/450 ml freshly squeezed lemon juice, strained

Preheat the oven to moderate, 350F/180C/gas mark 4.

Wipe the chicken pieces dry with kitchen paper, rub with salt and pepper and coat with flour. Heat oil in a large frying pan and fry the chicken, turning frequently until golden brown on all sides.

Lay the chicken pieces flat in a roasting pan or shallow oven-proof dish. Fit potato slices in all around, sprinkle over the garlic, herbs, salt and a great deal of black pepper, and pour over the lemon juice. Put to cook in the oven for $1\frac{1}{2}$–2 hours or till the potatoes are tender, the meat golden and the whole thing smells wonderful. If towards the end of the cooking time the dish seems to be drying out too much, turn the heat down a notch and sprinkle over a few tablespoons of water.

Serve with a classic Greek salad of tomatoes, olives, onion and cubes of feta cheese.

CHICKEN WITH FRUIT

Diana Huntley, antique dealer, Camden Passage

4 chicken pieces
oil
8 fl oz/225 ml chicken stock
small tin pineapple pieces
small tin mandarin pieces
1 oz/25 g butter

4 oz/125 g blanched almonds
2 oz/50 g maraschino cherries
1 teaspoon/5 ml curry paste
2 tablespoons/30 ml cornflour
4 fl oz/100 ml single cream

Fry the chicken pieces in the oil to brown skins. Place in a baking dish, pour over a small amount of stock and bake for 40 minutes at 400F/200C/gas mark 6, basting two or three times – add more stock if needed.

Make up stock to $\frac{1}{2}$ pint/250 ml with pineapple and mandarins and cherries.

When chicken is cooked, tip fruit and almonds over the chicken. Place back in oven while making sauce.

Put the stock in a saucepan, add a little cornflour and add remaining stock. Add curry paste and simmer for two minutes. Add the cream. Pour a little sauce over the chicken before serving, with the rest in a sauceboat.

Serve with rice.

PLUM DUCK

Andrew Mitchell, MP, Gedling.

Serves 4

4 duck breasts
salt and pepper
garlic, crushed
1¼lb/575 g red plums in syrup

2 teaspoons/10 ml Worcester sauce
1 tablespoon/15 ml wine vinegar
watercress to garnish

Set the oven at 400F/200C/gas mark 6.

Prick the skin of the duck breasts and rub in garlic, salt and pepper.

Place duck breasts in roasting tin and cook in pre-heated oven for 30 minutes.

Spoon off the fat, leaving the juices.

Mix juice of the plums, vinegar and Worcester sauce, salt and pepper. Make up to ½ pint/250 ml with water and pour over the duck. Cover with foil and cook for 45 minutes. Baste the duck and arrange plums around. Cook in oven for 15 minutes. Take off the foil for the last 10 minutes.

Put the duck in a serving dish with plums and watercress dressing. Spoon off excess fat from juice. Adjust seasoning and serve juice in a sauceboat.

DUCK SALAD

Emma Hope, shoe designer, Amwell Street.

Heat olive oil and brandy in a large pan. Fry halved kumquats and/or apricots with matchstick ginger and allspice. Add duck breasts, skin upwards. Add a slug of rice vinegar, 5 spice, spring onions, garlic and a little soy sauce.

To tell if it's done – thumb trick – *Rare*: like your palm when thumb is relaxed, *Medium*: palm with thumb firm, *Well done*: palm with thumb stretched.

Remove duck to grill to brown the skin. Add mushrooms to mixture in pan, and water if it's dry, add honey, balsamic vinegar. Cook through.

Put chicory leaves around a big bowl. Add cool duck, sliced into duck fingers, and put mushroom mixture into the middle.

CORONATION CHICKEN

Annette Ludvigsen, NSPCC Committee

Adapted from a Robert Carrier recipe.

Serves 6

1 large chicken (or 2–3 boneless chicken breast joints)
1 large carrot, washed and scraped
1 large onion, peeled and quartered
bouquet garni (tie together a few sprigs of parsley, rosemary and a large
    bay leaf)
salt and freshly ground pepper
1 tablespoon/15 ml sunflower oil
1 small onion, peeled and chopped
1 garlic clove, peeled and crushed
2 teaspoons/10 ml curry powder
1 teaspoon/5 ml tomato purée concentrate
3 fl oz/75 ml red wine
1 tablespoon/15 ml apricot jam
11 fl oz/330 ml mayonnaise (low calorie is fine)
2 fl oz/60 ml double cream, whipped
2 teaspoons/10 ml lemon juice

Put the chicken into a saucepan with the carrot, onion and bouquet garni, add salt and a good grinding of black pepper. Cover with cold water, bring to the boil and then lower the heat to simmer for about 1 hour (less if you are using boneless breast joints – 30 minutes). Leave to cool in the water as this will keep the meat moist. Remove the skin and then cut the meat into bite-size pieces.

Heat the oil in a small saucepan and sauté or fry the small onion and garlic gently until soft and translucent; do not brown. Add the curry powder and stir, cook for about 2 minutes, stir in the tomato purée, red wine and 2 fl oz/60 ml of water – simmer gently for about 10 minutes. Add the apricot jam and cook for a further 2–3 minutes. Cool completely.

Put mayonnaise into a bowl and sieve the curry mixture into it. Add the whipped cream and mix thoroughly. Season to taste and add lemon juice. Stir thoroughly, Add the chicken pieces and fold until fully incorporated. Serve with a green salad.

GLOUCESTERSHIRE PHEASANT

Sally Beauman, novelist

Serves 4

I call it this because that is where we tend to eat it, birds being cheap and plentiful in the country. It is quick and easy to prepare, and very good indeed.

2 hen pheasants that have been well hung (hen birds are more tender; underhung white birds are tough and useless)
$\frac{1}{4}$lb/125 g good unsalted butter
1 eating apple, peeled cored and sliced

For the sauce:
1 wine glass of alcohol – (fortified wines such as brandy or port or sherry are better than ordinary wines; if you have it, Calvados is best of all)
1 pint/500 ml good chicken stock
1 teaspoon/5 ml redcurrant jelly
juice of half an orange
salt and pepper to taste

Put butter and apple slices inside the pheasants, and butter the outside of them generously – they have a tendency to be dry. Place them in a roasting pan breast side down and roast them in a hot oven, 425F/220C/gas mark 7, for no more than 40 minutes. Turn them breast side up, and baste them with the buttery juices for the final 5 minutes of cooking time. Remove them from the pan, and allow them to rest in a gently warmed oven for at least 10 minutes – during this resting period you can make the sauce.

Pour off the fat from the roasting pan, but retain the juices. Over a high heat, deglaze the pan with your wine-glassful of brandy or Calvados, etc. Reduce the liquid, stirring constantly, until it has a thickish sticky consistency – do not allow it to burn. Add the stock, the juice from the half orange and the redcurrant jelly; add pepper to taste. Stir, and reduce over high heat until the sauce thickens slightly and tastes good – it should reduce by at least one third. Add salt to taste.

Serve the breasts of the pheasants, finely carved in thin slices, one breast per person (retain the rest of the birds for stock). They are delicious on triangular croutons of bread, fried golden in a mixture of olive oil and unsalted butter, dried in the oven. They are even better if the croutons have been spread with a dessertspoon/10 ml of finely diced game or chicken livers, previously sautéed in a little butter and oil, and cooked until pink. But this is not essential and, thanks to EC regulations, the pheasant livers are no longer easy to obtain.

Serve the sauce separately; tiny brussels sprouts and chestnuts go well with this.

PARTRIDGE IN A POT

Rodney Slatford, musician

If you live alone and hate Christmas, here's an alternative to turkey. It is enough for a special meal for one, or could be shared.

Heat some butter in a pan and brown the bird all over. Fry a chopped onion and place with the bird in the casserole. Then you can use your imagination. Any combination of mushrooms, celery, carrot and turnip can be added to the pot together with bits of fried bacon, or chestnuts, a clove or two, a bay leaf and some black pepper, some fresh thyme and parsley. For the liquid add orange juice, a little red wine and some good stock to cover the bird in the casserole. Try adding a cooking apple instead of the orange juice, or use a glass of port instead of the wine.

Cook in a slowish oven until the bird is tender (maybe 3–4 hours). If you have an Aga, of course, this sort of dish is a doddle! The meat will easily come away from the bones, depending on your cooking time. Any sort of oven-baked potato or mashed potato goes well with this, together with a green vegetable.

This dish is even better heated up the next day and any remnants can be liquidised for soup. I find I get carried away and add too many different ingredients, so maybe choose a few of those you can most easily get hold of and keep it simple. Thicken the sauce with anything you like.

SLOW COOKED GUINEA FOWL WITH POLENTA

Justin Cartwright, novelist

In South Africa there is a tradition of the pot-roast. There is also a widespread use of maize-meal, the sort of filling and cheap food which peasants around the world consume in one form or another. So I was pleased to find that these two elements come together in Italy in this dish, more usually served there with pheasant and rabbit, where it is known as *fagiano (or coniglio) stracotto*. It is very easy to make and elastic in its timing.

Serves 4

2 tablespoons/30 ml olive oil	1 tomato, skinned, diced and seeded
2 shallots, chopped	$\frac{1}{2}$ bottle Barolo or similar red wine
some diced chunks of ham	$\frac{1}{3}$ pint/185 ml chicken stock
1 guinea fowl	parsley, chopped
1 stick celery, chopped	1 tablespoon/15 ml tomato purée
large bunch herbs (favouring thyme and rosemary)	4–6 oz/125–175 g polenta

Take a chicken-shaped casserole dish, heat the olive oil, soften the chopped shallot in the olive oil, add the diced ham. When sizzling nicely, but before the shallots have burned, remove the ham and shallots with a slatted spoon and reserve. Now brown the guinea fowl thoroughly. Remove the guinea fowl. To the fat in the pan add the celery and the tomato and stir vigorously. Quickly add the wine and the chicken stock; reduce by fierce boiling for about 3 minutes. Take off the heat, season, place the guinea fowl in this, by now, brown and inviting liquid, add the herbs, shallots, ham and tomato purée previously stirred with some water. The guinea fowl should now be face down and two thirds submerged. Place in a low oven for $3\frac{1}{2}$ hours. Check to make sure it is only just bubbling.

Half an hour before serving, embark on the extremely easy task of making polenta like your mama would have if she had been Italian. You simply add water and a little salt to the polenta, stir from time to time, making sure it does not dry out, because polenta has an almost infinite capacity for absorbing water. Serve at a consistency like very firm porridge. (There are instant polentas in all Italian deli's.)

At this point, the guinea fowl will be falling off the bone. Remove it ready for carving, although little knife work is needed, remove the herbs and lumpy bits, reduce furiously for a few minutes, pour over the pleasantly tender bird and sprinkle with parsley. The polenta should also be libated in this way.

Serve with a salad of lightly blanched leaf spinach dressed, while still warm, with oil and lemon.

PIGEONS EN COCOTTE

David Simon, Chief Executive and Deputy Chairman, British Petroleum

This recipe is chosen to exhibit BP Chemicals, BP's and my own deep attachment to Europe and its culture . . .

Serves 4

4 pigeons	8 oz/225 g button mushrooms
1 oz/25 g butter	¾ oz/20 g plain flour
4 oz/125 g green streaky bacon	1 glass white wine
12 small button onions	7½ fl oz/200 ml chicken stock

Heat the butter in a deep pan, put in the pigeons and brown slowly on all sides. Set oven at 325F/170C/gas mark 3.

Cut bacon into lardons, peel onions and remove pigeons from the pan. Add bacon and onions, cook carefully until brown.

Remove bacon and onions from the pan with a draining spoon. Wash and trim mushrooms, cut in half and add to the pan. Cook until brown, remove from pan. Stir in flour, cook until golden brown, add the wine and stock, blend until smooth and bring to the boil.

Season and strain sauce into a bowl. Rinse and wipe out the pan, put back the pigeons, bacon, onions and mushrooms. Pour over sauce and bring to the boil. Cover tightly and cook in pre-set oven for approximately 2 hours until the pigeons are tender.

RABBIT CASSEROLE

John Murray-Brown, Angel Bookshop

This is a recipe from my favourite cookery book, Marcella Hazan's *Essentials of Classic Italian Cookery*, published by Macmillan. By tradition we have this dish every Christmas Eve.

1 rabbit (6–8 pieces)
6 tablespoons/90 ml olive oil
4 tablespoons/30 ml diced celery
clove garlic, crushed
$\frac{1}{4}$ pint/150 ml dry white wine
2 sprigs of rosemary
2 tablespoons/30 ml tomato purée
$\frac{1}{4}$ pint/150 ml stock

Take a rabbit which the butcher has cut up into 6 or 8 pieces and soak it overnight in cold water. Rinse and pat dry.

Put the pieces into a casserole with the olive oil and diced celery and garlic. Do not brown the meat but stew it gently over a very low heat.

After 2 hours, remove the lid, turn up the heat and simmer away the liquid which the meat has shed.

Finally, add the dry white wine, the rosemary and tomato purée dissolved in the stock, and reduce until the sauce is thick.

FILLET OF BEEF WITH CURRANTS	98	Chief Superintendent W.G. Sinclair, Metropolitan Police and Scotland Yard
FILLET OF BEEF	98	Christopher Newall, art historian
STEAK WITH MUSTARD AND TARRAGON	99	Siobhan Godfrey, Frank Godfrey Ltd, butchers
BEEF AND PEPPER HASH	100	Juliet Crocker, NSPCC Committee
SHREWSBURY LAMB	100	Rob Wood, psychotherapist
TASTY LEG OF LAMB	101	Gloria and James Elliott, Essex Road butchers
PERSIAN LAMB FILLETS	102	Sir Colin Davis, conductor
LAMB CHOPS ST PAUL'S ROAD	102	William Keegan, The Observer
SPECIAL LAMB/CHICKEN CURRY	103	Tony Allcock, editor, Islington Gazette
LAMB KEBABS WITH CORIANDER SAUCE	104	Jennifer Aykroyd, NSPCC Committee

MEAT

ROGNONS FLAMBE WITH SAFFRON RICE	106	Kenneth Pring, architect
PORK WITH RED CABBAGE	107	Penelope Lively, author
IRISH STEW	108	Anna Scher, Anna Scher Theatre
ROAST PORK WITH GARLIC	108	Anthony Delarue, architect
BECKENOF	109	Maryse Jones-Lassartesse, NSPCC Committee
PORK CHOPS WITH SOURED CREAM AND MUSHROOMS	109	Margaret Hodge, former leader of Islington Council
PORK WITH SAGE	110	Susan Bradshaw, concert pianist
YEAR OLD PIG'S BELLY	111	Stephen Cox, sculptor

FILLET OF BEEF WITH CURRANTS

W. G. Sinclair, Chief Superintendent, Metropolitan Police and Scotland Yard

Serves 2

2 oz/50 g currants
2 × 6–7 oz/175–200 g pieces of trimmed fillet
1 tablespoon/15 ml black peppercorns, crushed
2 oz/50 g butter
3 tablespoons/45 ml cognac
3 tablespoons/45 ml stock made with $\frac{1}{2}$ beef stock cube
salt

Bring $\frac{1}{2}$ litre water to boil and add currants. Boil for 5 minutes, drain and refresh under cold water.

Salt the beef and roll in the peppercorns, press into meat with palm of hand.

Heat a little butter and sauté beef on both sides for 2–3 minutes per side. Drain beef, set juices aside and keep hot in oven. Pour butter out of pan. Using same pan, put currants in, adding the cognac away from heat. Reduce over a low heat, then add stock. Simmer for 2 minutes without letting liquid reduce too much. Add remaining butter in small pieces and swirl into sauce. Add salt if necessary.

Arrange steaks and pour sauce over.

FILLET OF BEEF

Christopher Newall, art historian

Here's a standard for dinners of 8 or 10, according to the size of the fillet, and when you don't know at what time you are going to sit down and have little time to spare for final preparations.

Ask the butcher to cut the fillet into $1\frac{1}{2}$″ (4 cm) thick slices.

Fry the meat to seal it on all sides, and to cook it just on the outside.

Put the meat in the oven on a very low temperature when the first guest arrives.

To make the sauce:

Crush 2 cloves garlic, fry gently in a little butter but don't let it brown, add 4 oz/125 g chopped mushrooms (preferably including some fresh or dried ceps) and, when soft, stir in $\frac{1}{4}$ pint/150 ml cream.

Beef and sauce can each be left for an hour or so without being spoilt.

When the time comes, arrange the meat on a large plate and pour the cream and mushroom sauce over, adding, for a final touch, chopped parsley.

This is a standby of a fashionable and gregarious friend of mine. I have done it once or twice myself. Incidentally fillets can be bought extraordinarily cheaply at Smithfield any weekday morning, and there are a few stalls open on Saturdays.

STEAK WITH MUSTARD AND TARRAGON

Siobhan Godfrey, Frank Godfrey Ltd, butchers

Serves 4

2 tablespoons/30 ml fresh tarragon, chopped
4 tablespoons/60 ml French mustard
2 oz/50 g butter
1 clove garlic, peeled
4 sirloin steaks
$\frac{1}{2}$ pint/300 ml double cream
salt and black pepper
few splashes whisky or brandy

Mix tarragon with half the mustard and spread over the steaks, kneading it in all over. Cover and refrigerate for an hour to marinate. Melt butter in frying pan with garlic, add steaks and seal over a high heat, then continue cooking on a lower heat for the appropriate time ($2\frac{1}{2}$ minutes each side for rare, 4 minutes each side for medium, 6 minutes each side for well done for $\frac{3}{4}''$ (2 cm) thick steaks).

Remove meat to a separate serving dish and keep hot. Put remaining mustard and half the cream into the pan with the meat juices; heat slowly until it is quite hot, then add the rest of the cream and seasoning, and splash in whisky or brandy to taste. Serve the steaks with sauce, new potatoes and seasonal vegetables.

BEEF AND PEPPER HASH

Juliet Crocker, NSPCC Committee

Wonderful Texan way of dealing with left-over roast beef, this can also be made with minced or ground meat.

Serves 4

2 oz/50 g suet (or beef fat)	1 bay leaf
¾ cup boiled potatoes	salt and pepper to season
¾ cup green peppers, cut into chunks	3 tablespoons/45 ml Worcester sauce
½ cup onions	dash tabasco
½ cup celery, cut into chunks	½ cup canned tomatoes, crushed
½ teaspoon/3 ml thyme	4 cups beef, cubed or minced
½ teaspoon/3 ml oregano	1½ cups gravy

In a large deep saucepan heat the suet or fat until melted; about 10 minutes over a medium heat. Toss in the potatoes, the pepper, the onion and the celery, and cook until the onions are transparent. Stir in the herbs, seasoning and tomatoes. Add the beef and the gravy and cook over medium heat for 20 minutes. Correct the seasoning; Texans tend to lash in the tabasco although our delicate English palettes may stop short of gasping for breath!

Serve with wild grain rice and a large salad.

SHREWSBURY LAMB

Rob Wood, psychotherapist

This truly delicious English casserole is from, and for, my mother-in-law, Lois Child.

8 lamb cutlets (or 1½–2 lb/675–900 g chump or loin chops)
4 oz/125 g mushrooms
1 lemon
4 dessertspoons/40 ml redcurrant jelly
2 tablespoons/30 ml Worcester sauce
1 tablespoon/15 ml flour

$\frac{1}{2}$ pint/250 ml lamb stock
cooking oil
salt, pepper and nutmeg

Trim excess fat from meat and brown in a frying pan. Put in casserole and slice mushrooms over them. Keep the fat in the frying pan. Mix the lemon, redcurrant jelly and Worcester sauce in separate saucepan over a low heat. Brown flour in frying pan, stir in mixture from saucepan, stir in stock. Season with salt, pepper and a pinch of nutmeg. Pour over the meat and mushrooms. Cover and cook in oven at 325F/160C/gas mark 1 for 1$\frac{1}{2}$ hours. Serve with mashed potato.

TASTY LEG OF LAMB

Gloria and James Elliott, Essex Road butchers

Jim and I never have enough time to do elaborate preparation for a dinner party. We usually arrive home from the shop ten minutes before the guests appear, but we do enjoy good company. To that end all the dishes we present are easy to prepare, but tasty. Jim says that with first-class ingredients you don't need to disguise anything!

5 lb/2 kg leg of lamb, boned
home-made stock
vegetables, already cut chunkily, e.g. carrots, onions, swede, whatever you have
seasoning
potatoes

Fry lamb quickly to seal. Put in baking tin. Add stock to halfway. Add chunky vegetables. Place in oven at medium heat for 2$\frac{1}{2}$ hours. Slightly thicken stock to make gravy. Meanwhile chop potatoes into small cubes, add a little fat. Place at top of oven on high heat for 20–30 minutes.

Serve lamb sliced thinly with the crunchy potato cubes, fresh cabbage or greens, with the gravy.

PERSIAN LAMB FILLETS

Sir Colin Davis, conductor

Serves 2

4 lamb fillets (approx. 5″ (12 cm)) cut lengthways into strips

Marinade:
½ onion, grated   1 dessertspoon/10 ml olive oil
clove garlic   1 dessertspoon/10 ml sherry

Marinade the fillets for at least half an hour.

Grill. Pour sauce over grilled meat.

Sauce:
Chop a medium sized onion and 2 cloves garlic and fry in a knob of butter with 4 oz/125 g sliced mushrooms. Add 2 dessertspoons/20 ml soured cream and mix.

Serve with basmati or long-grained rice and a green vegetable.

LAMB CHOPS ST PAUL'S ROAD

William Keegan, The Observer

lamb chops, double-loin
onions
olive oil
pasta
tin tomatoes, peeled
tomato purée
herbes de Provence

Boil a kettle of water, light two rings and grill simultaneously. Boil pasta in one saucepan for 12 minutes. Cook sliced onions briefly in olive oil in a second saucepan, add one tin of tomatoes and a few dollops of tomato purée. Grill the chops, salted and with herbs on both sides.

Stir the onions/tomato mix frequently and thoroughly, at high temperature. Drain pasta after 12 minutes or so, and put into saucepan with tomatoes and onions and mix, cooking gently for a few minutes.

The whole thing takes 15 minutes, but don't forget to turn the chops over half way through.

SPECIAL LAMB/CHICKEN CURRY

Tony Allcock, editor, Islington Gazette

Lamb or chicken can be used, whichever is preferred.

Serves 4

1 large onion, sliced
curry powder (mix together these dry ingredients – 2 tablespoons/30 ml ready-made curry powder (Madras or Korma), 1 dessertspoon/10 ml garam masala, $\frac{1}{2}$ teaspoon/2.5 ml each ginger and cumin)
2 lbs/1 kg neck of lamb fillet or 4 chicken breasts
1 small tin tomatoes
4 oz/125 g mushrooms, sliced
2 fresh chillies, chopped small (do not discard seeds)
1 large tablespoon/15 ml tomato purée
2 dessertspoons/20 ml mango chutney
pinch coconut
3 tablespoons/45 ml natural yoghurt
small amount lemon juice

Fry sliced onion in a little oil until golden brown.

Add dry curry powders mixed together and fry with onion for about 3 minutes until forming a paste. Add chopped lamb pieces, or chicken breasts, to onions and curry powder and fry lightly until meat is sealed. Add chopped, tinned tomatoes, mushrooms, chillies and tomato purée. Stir all ingredients together and allow to cook for about 10 minutes. Add mango chutney and pinch coconut. It may be necessary to add a little water at this point if the sauce is becoming too thick. Allow to cook in pan with lid on for about $\frac{3}{4}$ hour. Remove from heat and stir in natural yoghurt, lemon juice and a little salt if necessary.

Serve with boiled rice.

LAMB KEBABS WITH CORIANDER SAUCE

Jennifer Aykroyd, NSPCC Committee

Serves 6

Ask your butcher to take out the bone from the top of a leg of lamb leaving you with about 2 lbs/900 g of fillet. You can ask him to cube the meat, but I prefer to do this myself so that they are all nice and square and measure about $1\frac{1}{2}''$ (4 cm).

Toss the cubes in a marinade and chill for at least 24 hours before serving. This makes the lamb very tender.

Yoghurt marinade:
1 pint/500 ml natural yoghurt
3 tablespoons/45 ml sunflower oil
3 tablespoons/45 ml fresh lime juice
1 teaspoon/5 ml each ground cloves, crushed cumin and ground cinnamon
about 15 crushed green cardamon seeds (don't worry if the husks get in too)
salt and pepper

When ready to serve, thread cubes on to skewers and cook on a grill or a barbecue for a maximum of 5 minutes either side, basting with some marinade. Push the meat off the skewers with a fork onto a serving dish and garnish with sprigs of coriander. Serve with new potatoes, mange tout or green salad and a coriander sauce.

Coriander sauce:
6 oz/175 g soured cream
1 tablespoon/15 ml oil
1 tablespoon/15 ml orange juice
dash of tabasco
salt and pepper
bunch of coriander, chopped (reserve some of the leaves for garnishing)

In a blender put the soured cream, oil, orange juice, tabasco, salt and pepper. Mix and pour into a bowl and add the coriander.

Ann Usborne July 1993

ROGNONS FLAMBE WITH SAFFRON RICE

Kenneth Pring, architect

This is an adaptation of a dish I once saw cooked many years ago in the
Portofino Restaurant in Camden Passage. I use a methylated spirit burner and a
copper frying pan lined with tin, but have also cooked this meal on a camping
gas stove, an electric and gas hob, and using an ordinary pan. It is preferable
if the food can be cooked and served at the table, as this allows the cook to
communicate with guests and provides an element of theatre to the meal.

Serves 4

8 lambs' kidneys, sliced	1 oz/25 g butter
salt and pepper	1 tablespoon/15 ml dry white wine
1 medium onion, chopped	cognac
parsley, chopped	1 dessertspoon/10 ml Dijon mustard
4 oz/125 g mushrooms, sliced	1 tablespoon/15 ml double cream

Skin kidneys and slice lengthwise. Snip out gristly areas with kitchen scissors
or use a sharp knife. Cut kidney slices into 3 or 4 pieces. Season with salt and
freshly ground pepper. Peel and finely chop onion. Wash, dry and chop
parsley. Remove stalks of mushrooms, wash or gently wipe as required and
slice.

At the table: melt butter in large frying pan, add onion and cook until opaque.
Put kidneys into the pan and turn until outside is browning, then add
mushroom slices; once these start to brown, add white wine – cook for a
minute or two, then add cognac – tilt pan to allow flame of the meths burner
to ignite the alcohol evaporating from the cognac. Once alight, agitate frying
pan to spread flame over the surface of kidneys and mushrooms. After
flaming, test kidneys to ensure they are nearly cooked to your taste, add
mustard, cream and parsley, and mix with the sauce formed by the kidneys,
butter, wine and cognac.

Serve with a flourish onto a bed of saffron rice.

A crunchy green salad is a good accompaniment.
Goes well with red, or chilled dry white wine.

Saffron rice:

2 pints/1 litre water	salt
generous pinch saffron	4 oz/125 g long grained rice

Boil the water with salt and saffron; I always use the strands of saffron rather than powder, as this gives a good flavour/colour and an attractive appearance to the rice. Add the rice and cook.

PORK WITH RED CABBAGE

Penelope Lively, author

$1\frac{1}{2}$ lb/675 g belly of pork, cubed
4 oz/125 g streaky bacon, rinded and cubed
1 large onion, peeled and chopped
1 clove garlic, crushed
1 large Cox's apple, sliced
2 tablespoons/30 ml oil
10 juniper berries, crushed
$\frac{1}{2}$ pint/250 ml dry cider
1 lb/450 g red cabbage, shredded
fresh parsley, chopped
salt and pepper

Set oven to 325F/160C/gas mark 3.

Soften onion and garlic in the oil.

Add bacon and pork cubes and brown on a high heat. Lower heat and add apple slices. Stir and after 5 minutes add the shredded cabbage and stir again. Then add juniper berries and cider.

Season and cook in oven for about 2 hours.

Decorate with chopped parsley.

It's hard to go wrong with this one, I find. Juniper berries can be hard to come by, but are essential, I fear. Classy delicatessens usually have them. Dried chestnuts are a very desirable addition – allow about 8 per person and soak overnight in white wine or dry cider. I sometimes skip the bacon – it can make the dish a bit fatty. And 2 or 3 tablespoons of red wine vinegar give it a nice kick.

IRISH STEW

Anna Scher, Anna Scher Theatre

I love Irish Stew. Well, I love anything Irish really, having left Cork, where I had the dubious distinction of being the only Jewish girl in an Irish convent, for Hove at the age of 14, an emotional age. Fond memories still linger three decades on of those convent days.

Irish Stew, strictly speaking, is an all-white affair as far as the vegetables are concerned:

Serves 2

2 lamb chops	1 leek	salt and pepper
2 onions	2 potatoes	a little chopped parsley
1 parsnip	2 teaspoons/10 ml pearl barley	$\frac{1}{2}$ cup vegetable stock or water

Simply prepare ingredients and lay in casserole dish with lamb chops at the bottom and potatoes on top. Pour on the stock, season with salt and pepper and bring to the boil. Place in the oven at 300F/150C/gas mark 2 for $1\frac{1}{2}$–2 hours.

To get the best results, cook in advance and reheat when required.

ROAST PORK WITH GARLIC

Anthony Delarue, architect

This is a Burgundian method which causes much surprise in England. Funnily, the garlic taste is not really noticeable, unlike in lamb.

Take a boned loin of pork (or a cheaper cut for the family) and fill the cavity beside the fillet with cloves of garlic, about 4 per lb. Roll and tie up. (You could just poke them in if your butcher ties the meat for you.)

Roast reasonably slowly, say 375–400F/190–200C/gas mark 5–6, for $\frac{1}{2}$ hour per lb. You could put herbs in too.

Because the garlic cuts the fat, you can serve this with quite a rich vegetable, such as a Gratin Dauphinois.

BECKENOF

Maryse Jones-Lassartesse, NSPCC Committee

This is an Alsatian dish, perfect for a cold winter evening.

Prepare lots of onions and potatoes cut in thin slices. Gently fry the onions. Put several layers of potatoes, then onions, then lamb (using an older lamb or chump chops), and pork (spare-rib) and carry on until you have your cooking pot nearly full, adding salt and pepper as you go along. Add parsley, rosemary, some home-made chicken stock and half a bottle of white wine. Cover the pot tightly with greaseproof paper or aluminium foil so that the steam does not evaporate.

Cook in the oven for $4 - 4\frac{1}{2}$ hours at 275F/140C/gas mark 1.

Serve with a garlicky winter salad, such as endive, apples and beetroot.

Bon appetit.

PORK CHOPS WITH SOURED CREAM AND MUSHROOMS

Margaret Hodge, former leader of Islington Council

This recipe emerged as a family favourite and an impressive tasty quick dinner dish for friends, after I used a bit of chef's licence with a recipe I learnt from my grandmother.

12 oz/350 g button mushrooms	paprika
butter	$\frac{1}{2}$ lemon
4 pork chops	1 pint/500 ml sour cream
salt and pepper	

Quarter the mushrooms and fry quickly in hot butter to seal them. Season the pork chops with salt, pepper, paprika and the juice of half a lemon. Fry the chops in butter until they are cooked and golden brown. Add the sour cream, mixing this in well with the juices in the frying pan. Add the mushrooms, season to taste and serve on a bed of rice.

Simple but delicious for the busy cook.

PORK WITH SAGE

Susan Bradshaw, concert pianist

The powdered sage gives this dish a hard-to-distinguish flavour all its own.
Quick to prepare – about 20 minutes – it is simple enough even for the least
practised cook!

1 medium onion
1 clove garlic
little flour
1 teaspoon/5 ml powdered sage
1 lb/450 g pork fillet
4 oz/125 g butter

2 oz/50 g sliced almonds
little light stock
salt and pepper
$\frac{1}{2}$ lb/225 g seedless grapes, cut in half
$\frac{1}{2}$ pint/250 g double cream

Chop onion and garlic. Combine flour and sage. Remove fat and gristle from
fillets, slice into thin rounds, then dust in flour and sage mixture. Melt some
of the butter in thick frying pan, add almonds and move around till lightly
brown; remove from pan and keep warm. Fry onions and fillet slices in
remaining butter, then add stock and cook quickly to reduce quantity by half.
Turn down heat, slowly add cream and seasoning, then grape halves and
almonds. Simmer for 5 minutes or so and serve with rice.

opposite: YEAR OLD PIG'S BELLY, *by Stephen Cox*

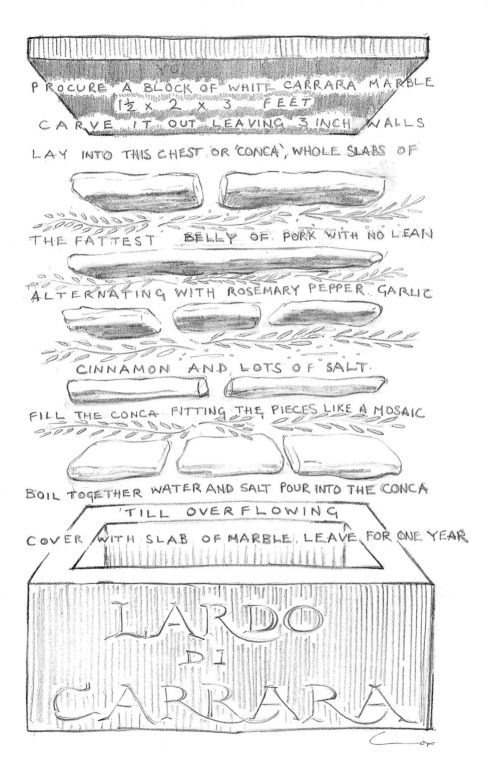

PROCURE A BLOCK OF WHITE CARRARA MARBLE
1½ x 2 x 3 FEET
CARVE IT OUT LEAVING 3 INCH WALLS

LAY INTO THIS CHEST OR 'CONCA', WHOLE SLABS OF

THE FATTEST BELLY OF PORK WITH NO LEAN

ALTERNATING WITH ROSEMARY PEPPER GARLIC

CINNAMON AND LOTS OF SALT.

FILL THE CONCA FITTING THE PIECES LIKE A MOSAIC

BOIL TOGETHER WATER AND SALT POUR INTO THE CONCA
'TILL OVERFLOWING

COVER WITH SLAB OF MARBLE LEAVE FOR ONE YEAR

LARDO
DI
CARRARA

A SIMPLE RECIPE FOR PORK   114   Susanna Cole, Cole & Son
(Wallpapers) Ltd.

EATING FOR ENGLAND – PIPERADE   114   Alastair Ross-Goobey, Chief Executive
of Postel

RACLETTE   116   Patricia Michelson, La Fromagerie,
Highbury Barn

HOME ALONE MEAT LOAF   117   Gemma Aykroyd, student

EMPANADA GALLEGA   118   Ange de Vena, NSPCC Committee

SALAD OF HOT POTATOES,   119   Rosemary Ruddle, cookery writer
BACON, ONIONS WITH ESCAROLE

POOR MAN'S SUPPER   120   Gawn Grainger, actor

IRISH CODDLE   120   Gawn Grainger, actor

RILLETTES   121   Rosemary Ruddle, cookery writer

SAUSAGES IN RED WINE   122   Betty Iles, Friends of Islington Libraries

TOAD IN THE HOLE   122   Dick Whetstone, Canonbury postman
and collector of historic postcards
of Islington

LUNCHES & SUPPERS

BIGOS (POLISH HUNTER'S STEW) 123 Helen Carpenter, 'Discover Islington'

CHEESE ON TOAST 124 Donald Trelford, former editor,
The Observer

SAVOURY SAUSAGE PIE 125 Canonbury Bookshop

SCRAMBLED EGGS AND BACON 126 David Rowland, Chairman, Lloyds

SWEETBREADS IN SOUR CREAM 126 Margaret Willes, publisher to the
National Trust

SPINACH AND CURD CHEESE PIE 127 Dr Ada Rapoport, Department
of Hebrew and Jewish Studies, UCL

COURGETTE AND PRAWN QUICHE 128 Jane Gibberd, headmistress,
The Children's House

FABULOUS FRENCH POTATO PIE 129 Mary Kleinmann, artist

VEGETABLE AND BACON STEW 129 Isabel Hilton, journalist

PILAFF 130 Sue Harris, music teacher

CHEESE SOUFFLE 131 Frances Cairncross, The Economist

A SIMPLE RECIPE FOR PORK

Susanna Cole, Cole & Son (Wallpapers) Ltd.

Coles Wallpapers has been producing hand-block printed wallpapers from its premises in Offord Road, Islington, since 1875.

4 slices of pork
1 small teaspoon/5 ml mustard
1 large teaspoon/6 ml honey
1 cooking apple
1 onion
pinch of salt
little pepper
squeeze of garlic (optional)
1 tablespoon/15 ml cornflour
milk and water to cover

Spread each slice of pork with mustard on one side and honey on the other and lay in a casserole. Cut up the apple and onion and spread over the pork. Add salt, pepper and garlic. Mix cornflour with a little milk and add milk and water. Pour over the pork slices.

Cook in oven until meat is soft, about $\frac{3}{4}$ hour.

EATING FOR ENGLAND

Alastair Ross-Goobey, Chief Executive of Postel

As an 11 stone 6 footer it is obvious that food does not have the central place in my life that drives other people to cooking and embonpoint. But over the years of travelling in pursuit of business and foreign trade I have had to eat some very odd things.

Japan is famous for its cuisine. Many a Brit has come to love raw tuna and miso soup, and is familiar with the differences between skiaki (not suki-yaki), shabut-shabu, yakitori, tempura and teppanyaki, even if they have not hazarded the dreaded fugu fish with its deadly poisonous liver. The Japanese show a remarkable indifference to what it is they are eating, and once, when I asked what was the particular piece of streaky bacon I was eating, the proprietress was driven to consulting her illustrated Japanese/English dictionary. After some time she presented me with the page and appropriate drawing; sea-slug ovaries. Just as well I didn't know that when they passed my lips.

In contrast to these delicate morsels the American plate groans with the size of the portions. On one occasion we were being entertained at Palm, a steak and lobster restaurant in New York, and were defeated by the size of the lobster. The waiter swept the substantial remnants into a doggy-bag and our hosts took us back to the hotel in their limo. We alighted, but the doggy-bag did not. A week later I was informed that our host had been forced to have his Mercedes fumigated as the ex-lobster made its presence known.

But the supreme test of the British stomach is Taiwan, where they seem to take great pleasure in testing the fortitude of the Westerner. I have had soup made from a very delicate part of a male frog's anatomy, and a fish which was served up in front of us looking complete, but which had been sliced like bread with a very sharp knife. Nobody had thought to tell the fish, so that periodically the whole body would twitch and the separate segments undulated in a particularly off-putting way.

For a more appetising prospect which was a frequent light Saturday lunch in our younger married days:

PIPERADE

Serves 2–3

Melt a little butter in a pan.

Chop an onion and a red pepper reasonably small.

Fry the onion and pepper until soft.

Meanwhile beat 4 eggs with milk, pepper and salt and pour over the onion and pepper.

Scramble eggs in the normal way.

Serve with crusty bread and cheese.

RACLETTE (Sunday roast with a difference)

Patricia Michelson, La Fromagerie, Highbury Barn

How often have you vowed never to cook Sunday lunch ever again? Slaving over a hot stove only to be told by recalcitrant teenage offspring that they're not hungry and want to sleep off Saturday night's rave; younger offspring hounding you because they have to be at a party at 3 pm sharp and, anyway, there will be lots of goodies to eat after the ear-bashing hour with Smarty Arty (you can imagine what that means, can't you!). Husband meanwhile is either playing golf/tennis/taking dog for walk to the pub, or some other pressing engagement, and will almost certainly arrive home, eat lunch and duly snore his way through to 6 pm. So the homely 'Oxo Cube' picture of happy British families passes into mythological realms. I suppose I am rather cynical, but after a hard week the last thing I want to do on Sunday is spend it entirely in the kitchen. So I have devised the perfect equivalent to the British Sunday Roast.

Raclette is a melting and scraping cheese from the Savoie region in France. If you go skiing you will have eaten it and, apart from the fact that it is dead simple to prepare, the group effort in assembling what actually goes on the plate is great fun. First, though, you should have a Raclette machine, which Tefal do in either 6 or 8 servings for table-top use. They are not outrageously expensive and are easy to clean. The Raclette cheese is cut to the size of the grilling plate and then placed inside the compartment where you can watch it sizzling away until it is ready. Everything is done at the table and the accompanying foods are prepared in moments. They consist of either steamed new potatoes or baked jacket potatoes, various salamis and perhaps air-dried Bresaola or venison, green salad or a mixture of your favourites, tiny cocktail gherkins, small sweet cocktail onions, crusty bread and a good French farmhouse butter. Vin chaud is a lovely accompaniment, and the children can have a spiced-up version of a hot blackcurrant drink; but a light fruity red Arbois wine or spicy white is good too, as well as a good quality dry apple juice such as James White's Bramley or their sweet Russet, which my kids adore.

Pudding can be a spicy apple pie with the addition of almonds – the pastry made beforehand and frozen, as indeed can the pie itself. Instead of serving cream, why not try a rich Normandy crème fraîche slightly sweetened with vanilla sugar, or Marscapone, the wonderfully rich Italian cream cheese, which is also faintly sweet.

Cooking at the table has always been great fun not only for the guests but for the hostess too. And certainly the Raclette Roast will be a relaxing and enjoyable way to deal with Sunday lunch.

HOME ALONE MEAT LOAF

Gemma Aykroyd, student

This recipe is ideal for teenagers who have been left to fend for themselves. It is quick, cheap, easy and very tasty.

Serves 4–6

1½ lb/675 g minced beef
½ lb/225 g sausagemeat (skin sausages yourself)
1 green pepper, finely chopped
1 large onion, finely chopped
3 slices crustless white bread soaked in milk and squeezed
1 teaspoon/5 ml dried mixed herbs
1 teaspoon/5 ml celery salt
1 teaspoon/5 ml French mustard
1 clove garlic, crushed
salt and pepper
Worcester sauce and tabasco

In a large bowl mix all the ingredients together very thoroughly and add as much Worcester sauce and tabasco as you can stand. Pack into a non-stick loaf tin 9″ × 5″ (25 × 13 cm) and cook for 1 hour at 350F/180C/gas mark 4. If the mince is cheap pour off any excess fat from time to time.

Turn out and serve sliced with jacket potatoes (baked at the same time) and tomato sauce made by heating oil in saucepan and adding 1 onion, roughly chopped, and 1 crushed clove of garlic. When softened, add one 15 oz/ 450 ml tin of chopped tomatoes, a pinch of dried basil, salt and pepper, and simmer for about 10 minutes to thicken.

EMPANADA GALLEGA Ange de Vena, NSPCC Committee

Serves 10

Dough:

10 handfuls of flour	1 tablespoon/15 ml yeast
3½ oz/100 g butter	1 teaspoon/5 ml salt
2 eggs	4 tablespoons/60 ml cold water

Filling:
3½ oz/100 g pork dripping, or olive oil
4 small onions
7 oz/200 g diced chorizo, without skin
18 oz/500 g pork, diced
7 oz/200 g cured ham, diced
7 oz/200 g steak, diced
1 red pepper
1 pinch cayenne pepper
1 egg yolk, beaten with 1 tablespoon/15 ml water and a pinch of saffron,
   salt and freshly ground black pepper

Make dough as if you were making bread, or you could use puff pastry instead.

In the meantime, heat the oil or dripping in a saucepan and fry the onions very gently. Add chorizo, pork, ham, steak, red pepper and cayenne, some saffron which has been ground in a mortar and seasoning to taste. Simmer for about 40 minutes until all the meat is tender.

Divide the dough in two and put one rolled half on a greased baking tray. Spread the filling over the dough leaving a ½" (1 cm) gap around the edges reserving 4 spoonfuls of juice to use later. Cover with other half of the dough and close it pressing well with fingers all around the edges. Brush all over with beaten egg. Finally, make some holes in the top to let the steam out.

Put empanada into a hot oven, 425F/220C/gas mark 7, for about 15 minutes until pastry is golden. Take out and pour reserved juice through holes.

Serve cold or hot with salad.

Spanish ingredients can be bought from 'Continental Touch'.

SALAD OF HOT POTATOES, BACON, ONIONS WITH ESCAROLE

Rosemary Ruddle, cookery writer

At the height of the 'nouvelle cuisine' movement, warm salads were fashionable. They had evolved from simple peasant salads like these. The preparation time is short, the flavours robust. Their success depends, not on culinary skill, but on buying good ingredients.

For this recipe from *The French Wine Harvest — Recipes and Traditions,* you need to track down some potatoes which the French use for salads because their texture is waxy, not crumbly. Some supermarkets now sell them, varieties such as Fir Apple Pinks, or Kipfler, small and long in shape.

1 lb/450 g potatoes
$\frac{1}{2}$ lb/225 g smoked or green streaky bacon in a piece
1 medium onion, or several shallots
escarole
oil and vinegar

Wash, but do not peel the potatoes. Cut each into about four, depending on size. Remove the rind of the bacon (it is used by thrifty French housewives for enriching a stew or stock) and dice. Peel and chop the onion or shallots.

Heat the pan and put in the diced bacon. Let the fat melt and sauté the potatoes and onion in it. Keep stirring and scraping the bottom of the pan, so everything becomes crispy without burning. If you feel the bacon has not given enough fat, add some oil. The smell is wonderful and everyone will be very pleased to eat as soon as you mix the contents of the pan with the escarole, washed, dried and dressed lightly with oil and vinegar, ready in a bowl large enough to allow you to turn everything vigorously.

POOR MAN'S SUPPER

Gawn Grainger, actor

Serves 2–4, depending on how hungry you are! For more, simply
add to the amounts.

2–4 potatoes, sliced thick as for crisps
1 small cabbage, sliced or shredded
½lb/225 g off cuts of bacon
½lb/225 g grated cheese

In a casserole or heat-proof dish place a layer of potatoes, cover it with a layer
of cabbage, followed by a layer of bacon, topped by a layer of cheese.
Repeat the procedure until you reach the top of the pot. Place in a low oven,
275F/140C/gas mark 1, and cook for 1½ hours.

The smell is outrageous, the taste fantastic, the children love it and it is
simplicity itself. Must be if I can do it!

IRISH CODDLE

Gawn Grainger, actor

Serves 2

4 thick sausages
½lb/225 g off cuts of bacon
1 large onion, cut lengthways
2 medium potatoes, rough cut
1 pint/500 ml stock, or water

Casserole the lot!

Cook over a medium heat for half an hour.

Ten minutes before ready, add 1 tablespoon/15 ml cornflour mixed in a cup
of milk. Finish cooking, adding salt and pepper to taste.

RILLETTES

Rosemary Ruddle, cookery writer

(From The French Wine Harvest – Recipes and Traditions)

Large bowls of this soft, melting kind of potted pork or pâté are in every charcuterie in the Loire. A fine example of the French knack for turning cheap ingredients into something delicious, it is easy to make at home.

2 lb/900 g belly or neck of pork, rind and bones removed
1 lb/450 g back of pork fat
1 clove garlic
bouquet garni of parsley, thyme and bay leaf
salt and pepper
little water

Cut the meat into short strips about the width of a finger. Cut up the back fat roughly. Put all into a casserole with the garlic, herbs, salt and pepper and water just to cover the bottom of the pan. Put on the lid and cook in a very slow oven, 280F/140C/gas mark 1, for about 4 hours.

It cannot be said to look very appetising at this stage. The next step is to drain off the fat and keep it. Throw away the bouquet garni. Pound the meat in a pestle and mortar for a few minutes. The meat is soft and the job is easy. Resist the temptation to use a food processor – it ruins the texture which should not be that of a smooth paste. Finally, take two forks and pull the pork into shreds. You end up with a pale mushroomy-pinky-brown mass of meat marbled with deeper pink streaks. Taste for seasoning – rillettes should not be bland.

Traditionally rillette pots are like rather thick, salt-glaze, earthenware mugs, but any earthenware or china pot or bowl will do. Whatever you choose, pile the mixture into it without pressing it down into a compact paste. Pour the melted fat you put aside earlier over the top. Rillettes will keep well in a larder or fridge sealed by the fat and covered with foil. Remember to take them out of the fridge in good time so that they are soft, to spread on fresh bread and enjoy with a glass of Vouvray or other fruity Loire wine.

Rillettes de Lapin – a variation.

Harvest cooks use a lot of rabbit – many families raise them for eating. Use $\frac{1}{2}$ lb/225 g rabbit to $1\frac{1}{2}$ lbs/675 g of pork and proceed as before.

SAUSAGES IN RED WINE

Betty Iles, Friends of Islington Libraries

Serves 4

2 tablespoons/30 ml oil
1 lb/450 g pork sausages
$\frac{1}{2}$ lb/225 g lean bacon, cubed
$\frac{1}{2}$ lb/225 g button onions
6 oz/175 g button mushrooms, halved
1 dessertspoon/10 ml flour
clove of garlic, finely chopped
1 bay leaf
$\frac{1}{2}$ teaspoon/2.5 ml dried thyme or 1 teaspoon/5 ml fresh
salt and pepper
$\frac{1}{2}$ pint/300 ml red wine

Heat the oil in a frying pan and gently brown the sausages. Transfer them to a casserole dish. Fry the bacon and onions until lightly coloured. Add the mushrooms and cook for 5 minutes. Sprinkle in the flour and cook for 1 minute. Add garlic, herbs and freshly ground black pepper. Go easy on the salt. Add half the wine and stir. Pour contents of the pan over the sausages. Rinse the pan with the rest of the wine and add to the dish. Cover with a lid and cook for 1 hour.

TOAD IN THE HOLE

Dick Whetstone, Canonbury postman and collector of historic postcards of Islington

Serves 4

1 tablespoon/15 ml oil
1 lb/450 g pork sausages

Batter:
$\frac{1}{4}$ pint/150 ml milk
$\frac{1}{4}$ pint/150 ml water
1 egg
4 oz/125 g plain flour
salt and pepper

Place the oil in a shallow ovenproof dish, about 8″ × 12″ (20 × 30 cm). Arrange the sausages in it. Cook in a pre-heated hot oven, 425F/220C/gas mark 7, for 10 minutes. Place the batter ingredients in the blender and blend for 30 seconds. Lower the oven temperature to 400F/200C/gas mark 6. Pour the batter over the sausages and cook for 25–30 minutes until well risen and golden brown.

BIGOS (POLISH HUNTER'S STEW)

Helen Carpenter, 'Discover Islington'

This stew was originally kept in barrels and buried for hunters to dig up and eat in winter. It has adapted remarkably well to the modern kitchen and works best if made in a slow cooker. Like pease pudding, it improves with keeping!

1 lb/450 g jar of sauerkraut
1 lb/450 g white cabbage, finely chopped
1 lb/450 g cooking apples, peeled and chopped
1 oz/25 g dried mushrooms
2 large onions, chopped
butter or margarine, or lard, or bacon fat
1 ½ lb/675 g various meat, roughly chopped, eg garlic ring sausage, bacon
   or bacon bits, remainders of any roast meat (pork or beef), ham, etc.
pitted prunes (about 1 dozen)
caraway seeds
salt and pepper

Add very little water to sauerkraut and cabbage and cook at very low heat until soft. Stir in cooking apples and continue to cook for a few minutes. Cook dried mushrooms in a little water during this time, slice finely and add to mixture. Meanwhile in another pan, brown the chopped onions in butter (lard or bacon fat are traditionally used). Bacon, if used, must be chopped and fried with the onion. When the onion is ready, add to the cabbage mixture with all the chopped meats and the prunes. Season with salt, pepper and caraway seeds. If the stew seems very solid, add a little water or red wine to moisten. Transfer to a large casserole and cook for at least 1 ½ hours at a very slow heat in the oven, or for at least 6 hours in a slow cooker.

After cooking, leave to rest and reheat as required. The dish improves with each reheating. It also keeps very well in the freezer.

CHEESE ON TOAST

Donald Trelford, former editor, The Observer

My lack of interest in culinary matters is legendary. When I first left home for Cambridge, nostalgia for my mother's sweet cooking prompted me to make jellies – a task well within my range. I left them to set underneath my bed, where they acquired a dusty tang I still savour in my memory. My father, who used to pay my college buttery bill with good grace, couldn't help noticing that my diet seemed to consist almost entirely of Madeira, Yugoslav Riesling and chocolate biscuits.

Later on I developed a way with curry. This I have now forgotten. However, I occasionally offer unsolicited (and not altogether welcome) advice to my wife on the benefits of adding raisins or bananas at the right moment.

Once or twice I have been known to produce roast lamb under minute-by-minute instruction over the car telephone as the recipients draw nearer. I once made a serious error, having ignored my wife's instructions to leave the peas until she arrived. I thought defrosting would help. Pity it was a 5 lb bag. I draw the line at gravy.

Left on my own, I sink as low as baked beans. On one occasion my wife had taken the best tin-opener to a country cottage and left me with a new-fangled gadget which instruction by telephone failed to explain sufficiently. Having resorted to every tool I could lay my hands on, including a hammer and chisel, and used every expletive known to man, I eventually made a hole big enough to extract the beans one at a time.

So really it has to be: Cheese on Toast.

Take 2 slices of bread (white if available, tho' sadly it rarely is in my household). Place on grill and while first side is browning, prepare slices of cheese from any lurking in the fridge. I prefer mouse-trap Cheddar and Red Leicester. When the toast is ready to turn, do so and arrange slices of cheese (not too thick) on the untoasted side. If arranged as a chess board, the final effect is attractive. Place under the grill until the cheese bubbles.

This goes down well with lager, red wine or coffee, depending on mood or time of day.

SAVOURY SAUSAGE PIE

Canonbury Bookshop

Pastry:
8 oz/225 g plain flour
5 oz/150 g fat of your choice
water to mix

4 streaky rashers, finely chopped
1 medium-sized onion, finely chopped
1½ lb/675 g pork sausagemeat
2 oz/50 g sultanas
1 tablespoon/15 ml sage, finely chopped
½ teaspoon/2.5 ml dry mustard
black pepper to taste
1 egg, separated
1 large cooking apple

In a frying pan, cook bacon until fat starts to run, add onion and cook until soft but not brown. Remove from pan and dry on kitchen paper.

Mix bacon, onion, sausagemeat, sultanas, herbs and seasonings together and form to fit 6–7″ (15–18 cm) tin (it will shrink a little). Place mixture on a piece of foil on a baking sheet and cover with a piece of grease-proof paper. Cook in pre-heated oven, 400F/200C/gas mark 6, for 20 minutes (this allows the surplus fat to run).

Meanwhile line tin with pastry, using the white of egg to seal joins. Peel, core and grate apple and spread over pastry in bottom of container. When slightly cool, place sausagemeat in tin, cover and seal with pastry. Brush top with egg yolk. Bake for 40 minutes at 400F/200C/gas mark 6.

This recipe works well if made into a sausage plait.

SCRAMBLED EGGS AND BACON

David Rowland, Chairman, Lloyds

I can only cook toast, scrambled eggs and bacon. Fortunately all three go together. Incredible skill is required to produce the perfect combination. Usually conditions for this are only right on Sunday evenings. Timing is crucial. The toast must be warm and buttered, the bacon crisp and hot and the eggs ... but that is where the real skill comes in. Let me explain.

Take 2 eggs per person – they must be fresh and brown (I don't like white eggs). Break them into a bowl. Usually I can't find a bowl so I use my wife's giant coffee cup. Add salt and pepper to taste – which always means more than you think – and whisk lightly with a fork. No milk must be added in any circumstances; this produces a quite horrible substitute for really delightful scrambled eggs. Put an ample supply of rashers of streaky bacon into a frying pan. Heat slightly to begin with and then fiercely until crisp. At the same time warm a lump of butter in a wide saucepan. Put the toast in the toaster. Put the eggs in the saucepan and stir continuously with a wooden spoon. Shout for your wife – in my case for my wife as I suddenly realise I can't watch the bacon, stir the eggs, rescue the toast and butter it! In a state of confusion the toast is buttered, bacon is crisp and eggs served ... just at that moment before you think they are ready, because in the time that you take the saucepan from the stove they go on cooking.

Then bask in the warm admiration of your wife for the extraordinary culinary skills that you have displayed.

Wait until next Sunday before trying again.

SWEETBREADS IN SOUR CREAM

Margaret Willes, publisher to the National Trust

I'm one of those inquisitive people who sees something new in a shop, buys it and then has to discover how to cook it. I found lambs' sweetbreads in the excellent butchers that used to be in the Blackstock Road in Highbury. Only when I got them home did I start to investigate what to do with them. I cannot stand coating them in breadcrumbs – that seems to take all the moisture and texture out of them. As all my books could only suggest this method, I made one up for myself. It may have a fancy name and be the brainchild of Eliza Acton or Francatelli, in which case it was serendipity.

Go for lambs' rather than calves' sweetbreads because they are smaller and tenderer. To prepare them, you blanch them quickly in boiling water, then put in cold water. Remove the skins and any bits of membrane and gristly bits.

Serves 2

8 oz/225 g sweetbreads
8 oz/225 g button mushrooms
2 oz/50 g butter
$\frac{1}{4}$ pint/150 ml soured cream (crème fraiche will work too, but not yoghurt)
salt and black pepper
parsley to garnish

Cut the sweetbreads into approx. 1″(2.5 cm) cubes, and the mushrooms to about the same size – they should be chunky rather than sliced. Melt the butter in a heavy-bottomed frying pan, add the sweetbreads and mushrooms and cook for about 5 minutes. Add cream to give a sauce-like consistency, and cook for another 5 minutes. Season to taste with ground black pepper and salt, and garnish with chopped parsley.

Serve with rice and a green salad to complement the very delicate taste.

SPINACH AND CURD CHEESE PIE

Dr Ada Rapoport, Department of Hebrew and Jewish Studies,
University College London

A large pie serves approx. 12 portions

2 (or even 3, for a thicker pie) packets frozen chopped spinach
2–3 large onions
3 lb/1.35 kg curd cheese
6 eggs
salt
a lot of black pepper
frozen puff pastry (either one packet of 5 already flattened sheets or two
    standard size rectangles)

Cook the spinach (from frozen) in a large pan without any additional water, starting on a low fire with the lid on and eventually, when all the ice has melted and the spinach is soft, on a high flame, with the lid off, stirring frequently to prevent burning, until all the water has evaporated. The drier the spinach, the better the pie (the alternative method is to cook the spinach until all the ice has melted and then drain it in a sieve, but this takes a very long time).

Chop the onions very small and put in a large bowl. Add the curd cheese, the eggs, plenty of salt and pepper, and mix well. Add the spinach (once it has cooled a little) and mix evenly. Pour the mixture into a large, oiled, baking tin. Join the pastry rectangles together and roll them to make one large piece. Stretch it over the mixture, squeezing along the edges to seal. With the point of a sharp knife and a light touch, mark a grid on the pastry, to prevent it from bursting in the oven.

Cook in the oven, 375–400F/190–200C/gas mark 5–6, until the pastry is brown. For easier slicing and a more solid pie, pre-cook until pastry begins to brown, take out and cool, completing the cooking some 30–45 minutes before serving.

COURGETTE AND PRAWN QUICHE

Jane Gibberd, headmistress, The Children's House

Serves 4

8 oz/225 g shortcrust pastry
3 eggs
7 oz/200 g cream cheese with garlic and herbs
4 oz/125 g courgettes
4 oz/125 g prawns, shelled
pinch of dill or parsley
salt and pepper

Line a 9″(23 cm) flan tin with pastry and bake blind at 375F/190C/gas mark 5 for 20 minutes. Beat together the eggs and cream cheese and add the grated courgettes and prawns. Add seasonings.

Pour into flan dish and bake for 30 minutes or until set.

FABULOUS FRENCH POTATO PIE Mary Kleinman, artist

Serves 4

1 lb/450 g pastry (your preference)
2 lbs/900 g potatoes, peeled and thinly sliced
parsley, lots, and roughly chopped
approximately 1 oz/25 g butter
1 cup double cream

Line greased baking dish with three-quarters of the pastry. Alternate layers
of potato sprinkled with salt and pepper, dotted with butter and the parsley.
Cover with remaining pastry and bake for 1 hour in a fairly hot oven,
375F/190C/gas mark 5.

Ceremonially cut a window in the pastry lid and trickle in the cream. Replace
the pastry.

Serve very hot.

Accompany with a light salad and a glass of wine. A meal in itself.

VEGETABLE AND BACON STEW

Isabel Hilton, journalist

$\frac{1}{2}$ lb/225 g butter beans, soaked overnight
3 leeks
1 clove garlic
1 onion

5 potatoes, peeled and sliced
3 rashers bacon, cut in strips
seasoning (including cumin)

Cook the butter beans in ham stock for $\frac{1}{2}$ hour.

Slice the leeks, onions, garlic and potatoes.

Fry bacon strips, add a little oil and sauté the vegetables together.

Add beans and stock (and more water if needed).

Cook until tender; add seasoning, herbs and cumin.

Serve with fresh brown bread.

PILAFF

Sue Harris, music teacher

Serves 4–6

A much-loved weekly favourite in our household.

Melt a good 1 lb/450 g of sliced onion in butter and a little oil in a large wide shallow pan with a lid. Add 2 cloves of garlic, chopped. Meanwhile cut up the cooked meat left over from your latest roast into smallish pieces, most delicious with chicken, pork or lamb (not beef!). Slice any bits of left-over salami, ham or cooked sausages you may find in your fridge. Add this chopped, cooked meat to the onions when they are golden. Throw in a generous handful of currants and a tin of chopped tomatoes with peppers. Sometimes I add some peas, or a little chopped celery or shredded cabbage at this stage. Season well with salt, black pepper and plenty of nutmeg. Stir around, cover and simmer gently with the lid on.

Have cooking 2 good cups of brown rice – more or less depending on how much meat mixture you have. When the rice is cooked, drain and put straight into a large heated, shallow serving dish. Add the meat and onion mixture and mix thoroughly with the rice – the result should be a fairly moist, colourful mound. Serve with fresh natural yoghurt to spoon on top of each helping and a crisp green salad.

Robin Richmond

CHEESE SOUFFLE

Frances Cairncross, The Economist

Serves 4

$1\frac{1}{2}$ oz/40 g butter or margarine	salt, pepper and a pinch of English mustard
2 oz/50 g flour	6 oz/175 g strong Cheddar cheese, grated
$\frac{3}{4}$ pint/400 ml milk	4 eggs

Heat the butter in a saucepan and stir in the flour with a wooden spoon.
Add the milk gradually, and stir till thick and smooth. Season with salt, pepper
and mustard. Stir in the cheese. Cool to lukewarm.

Separate the eggs. Stir yolks into the mixture, one at a time beating hard after
each. Stiffly beat the egg whites, fold into the mixture and pour into a
buttered soufflé dish. The soufflé will rise better if you warm the dish first.
Bake at 350F/180C/gas mark 4 for 15 minutes. Turn up the heat to 450F/
230C/gas mark 8 and bake for a further 15 minutes. Eat at once – a soufflé
won't wait!

ISLINGTON CHEESECAKE	134	Marian Harvey and Mary Cosh, The Islington Society
VANILLA CRESCENTS	135	Dr. Anna Skalicka, GP
BRANDY CROISSANT PUDDING	135	Thane Prince, cookery writer
POACHED PEARS WITH TWO SAUCES	136	Audrey Knight, Mange Tout – Highbury Caterers
RHUBARB FOOL	137	Margaret F. Chittick, retired director, Islington Sixth Form Centre
APPLE CHEESECAKE	137	Stephen Fry, actor and writer
SULTANA SPONGE TART	138	Tim Coulson, headteacher, William Tyndale Primary School
MACGREGOR'S ATHOLE BROSE	139	Roy MacGregor, GP TVam doctor
KATRINA'S APPLE CAKE	140	Lisa Appignanesi, writer
BANANA FOOL	140	Alex Forshaw, Islington's Conservation Officer
FLO'S DELICIOUS 'AFTER THE SHOW' BREAD PUDDING	141	Flo Jeffries, The Little Angel Marionette Theatre
MULBERRY MOUSSE	141	Fiona Boyle, administrator, The Tower Theatre
BANANA SOYA DESSERT	142	Chuka and Dubem Okonkwo, The Highbury Twins
CREME BRULEE	142	Linda Gumb, antique dealer, Camden Passage
SOUR CREAM CAKE	143	Susan Barrie, hairdresser
BAKED FUDGE PUDDING	143	Dennis Marret, barber, Huckers

PUDDINGS

DUTCH APPLE PIE	144	Marianne Fox Ockinga, artist
MAUD'S CHOCOLATE PUDDING	144	Canonbury Bookshop
LEMON CHEESECAKE	145	Allan's Shoe Shop
AN ABUNDANCE OF APRICOTS	146	Mary Kleinman, artist
INDIAN PUDDING	148	Ann Usborne, artist
PUFF PASTRY YUM YUM	149	Annie Williams, artist
MINT ICE CREAM AND MINT SAUCE	149	Jennifer Vernor-Miles, NSPCC Committee
PEACH MOUSSE	150	The Continental Touch, Spanish delicatessen
PASSION CAKE	150	Gill Wing, Le Café
APPLE AND MINCEMEAT STEAM PUDDING	151	The Albion Pub
LEMON DELICIOUS	151	Granita's Restaurant
MOTHER'S CHRISTMAS PUDDING	152	Diana Matthews, estate agent
CRUNCHIE BAR ICE CREAM	153	Greg Coad, Islington Majestic Wine Warehouse
TARTE TATIN	153	Gerald Harper, actor
FRUITS BRULES	154	Nigel Slater, cookery writer
BANANA FLAMBE	155	David Gibson, architect
FRUITS CLAFOUTIS	155	Muriel Feder, NSPCC Committee
BREAD AND BUTTER PUDDING	156	Katharine Hamnett, fashion designer

ISLINGTON CHEESECAKE

Marian Harvey and Mary Cosh, The Islington Society

The Islington Society's contribution is the traditional Islington cheesecake, from a recipe circulated by the Council a couple of years ago.

In its merry days of pleasure gardens and spas, Islington was renowned not only for pure spring water but for fresh milk from its large dairy farms. One of the delicacies sampled by those who flocked here for an evening's recreation was a rich cheesecake made from local cream. This version is slightly modified, with a few up-to-date substitutes, if you want to compromise a little.

1 lb/450 g rolled-out short pastry
3 oz/75 g butter, unsalted
3 oz/75 g Demerara sugar
1 lb/450 g curd cheese (or cottage cheese, or Quark)
$\frac{1}{2}$ pint/250 ml double cream
3 eggs
2 oz/50 g currants
1 oz/25 g ground almonds (optional)
2 fl oz/60 ml Madeira or cream sherry
pinch of nutmeg and cinnamon
zest of 1 orange and 1 lemon
juice of $\frac{1}{2}$ lemon

Line a large flan ring (or two 9″(23 cm) flan rings) with the pastry.

Bake blind, and allow to cool.

Beat butter and sugar until soft.

Add all other ingredients – curd cheese, cream, lightly beaten eggs, currants, almonds, Madeira and flavourings, and mix well.

Pour mixture into flan rings. Bake at 300F/150C/gas mark 2 for 30–40 minutes, until firm to touch and golden brown on top.

Allow to cool, and remove from flan ring.

Preferably chill before eating.

(N.B. It can also be frozen.)

VANILLA CRESCENTS

Anna Skalicka, GP

A recipe from Czechoslovakia

8 oz/250 g flour
7 oz/210 g butter
4 oz/100 g ground walnuts (or mixture of walnuts and almonds)
3 oz/75 g caster sugar

Make into a smooth pastry (can be done in a food processor) and allow to rest in a cool place for 10–15 minutes. Form a roll, cut off small pieces and shape them into small crescents. Place them on a greased tin and bake in a moderate pre-heated oven, 325F/160C/gas mark 3, until pink. Remove carefully and roll crescents in the remainder of the caster sugar (ie. a very little) which has been flavoured by adding 2 or 3 drops of vanilla essence.

BRANDY CROISSANT PUDDING

Thane Prince, cookery writer

This wonderfully light pudding puffs up like a soufflé and tastes delicious.

4 oz/125 g day-old croissants
1 tablespoon/15 ml chopped candied peel
$\frac{3}{4}$ pint/375 ml creamy milk
2 × size 2 eggs
2 oz/50 g caster sugar
$\frac{1}{2}$ teaspoon/2.5 ml vanilla essence
1–2 tablespoons/15–30 ml brandy
butter
granulated sugar

Butter an ovenproof dish. Slice the croissants and arrange in the dish sprinkling the candied peel over evenly. Beat the milk, eggs, sugar, vanilla essence and brandy together and pour over. Leave for 1–2 hours. Dot pudding with butter and sprinkle with a little granulated sugar. Bake in a pre-heated oven, 350F/180C/gas mark 4, for 45–60 minutes, or until golden brown. Serve warm with cream.

POACHED PEARS WITH TWO SAUCES

Audrey Knight, Mange Tout, Highbury Caterers

Serves 4

7 oz/200 g sugar
1 pint/500 ml water
1"(2.5 cm) piece of fresh ginger, peeled
1 lemon
4 pears, peeled, halved and cored

Dissolve sugar in the water and bring to boil. Add fresh ginger and the juice of the lemon. Turn heat down and simmer until the pears are tender.

Caramel cream sauce:
Place 3 oz/75 g sugar in a mound in a thick-bottomed pan with 2 tablespoons/30 ml water round the sugar. Place over low heat and melt slowly tipping the pan from time to time. If necessary brush the sides of the pan with cold water to dissolve any sugar crystals. (If there are any undissolved sugar crystals when the sugar starts to boil it will not caramelise properly). Boil the sugar until it is a dark golden brown colour. Remove from the heat. Bring 5 fl oz/125 ml of double cream to the boil and pour it into the caramel. Stir over low heat until caramel is dissolved into the cream.

Chocolate sauce:
Melt 6 oz/175 g plain chocolate gently in 3 fl oz/90 ml water with 1 teaspoon/5 ml of sugar. Then add 2 oz/50 g butter and 1 dessertspoon/ 10 ml golden syrup.

Let pears cool in the syrup. Place two halves on each plate and pour chocolate sauce round one side and caramel cream sauce round the other.

Alternatively a scoop of chocolate ice cream (homemade, or the very best bought varieties) placed in the scooped-out cores of the pears and surrounded with caramel cream sauce is delicious.

RHUBARB FOOL

Margaret F. Chittick, retired Director, Islington Sixth Form Centre 1986–1993

From the 'Working Woman's Pact', Odham's Leisure Group.

13½ oz/380 g can of rhubarb
1 tablespoon/15 ml orange juice
½ pint/250 ml whipping cream
½ teaspoon/2.5 ml ground ginger

Place rhubarb and orange juice in a liquidiser and blend for 1 minute.

Whip cream until stiff and fold in the ginger and rhubarb mixture.

Spoon into individual dishes and place in fridge for at least 1 hour until required.

APPLE CHEESECAKE

Stephen Fry, actor and writer

6 oz/175 g shortcrust pastry
2 eggs, separated
2 oz/50 g sugar
8 oz/225 g cream cheese
5 fl oz/125 ml sour cream
3 tablespoons/45 ml apple purée, slightly sweetened

Roll out pastry and use to line a 7″ (18 cm) cake tin. Cover and chill in the fridge for 30 minutes.

Whisk egg yolks with sugar until pale, light and creamy. Beat cream cheese vigorously until smooth and fold in. Stir in sour cream and then add to the apple purée. Whisk egg whites until stiff, then carefully fold into the mixture using a metal spoon.

Retrieve the pastry-lined tin from the fridge and fill with the apple and cream cheese mixture. Bake in a pre-heated oven at 350F/180C/gas mark 5 for 45 minutes, or until filling is firm and set, and pastry is crisp.

SULTANA SPONGE TART

Tim Coulson, Headteacher, William Tyndale Primary School

Many of my favourite meals are those served up for school meals. Four days out of five I thoroughly enjoy and am a strong advocate of school meals (the fifth day is a roast, in which the meat is a strong advertisement for becoming a vegetarian). I am also extremely fond of anything made in our nursery class. Enough of this preamble, my absolute favourite recipe is getting up early on Christmas morning and spending all morning preparing dinner for a large group. An easier recipe to transcribe, however, is that of this delicious sultana sponge tart.

Filling:	4 oz/125 g sultanas
1 oz/25 g margarine	1 level teaspoon/5 ml plain flour
1 oz/25 g soft brown sugar	pinch ground cinnamon

Make the filling first. Put all the ingredients into a saucepan and, over a low heat, bring the mixture to the boil, stirring all the time. Leave on one side to cool.

Pastry:	
5 oz/150 g plain flour	1 oz/25 g margarine
pinch salt	1 oz/25 g lard

Make pastry in whatever way you find best. I sieve the flour and salt into a mixing bowl, add the fat (cut into small pieces) and rub them in. Stir in water to make a firmly stiff dough. Roll a circle larger than the flan ring and press it into the base and sides.

Sponge topping:	
1 large egg	2 oz/50 g caster sugar
2 oz/50 g margarine	2 oz/50 g self-raising flour

Put the egg, margarine, sugar and flour into mixing bowl and beat with a wooden spoon to ensure air gets into the mixture. Spread filling over flan case and cover this with the sponge mixture.

Roll out any scraps of pastry and cut them into six strips. These are placed in a lattice on top of the tart. Bake at 375F/190C/gas mark 5 for 40 minutes or until pastry is golden brown and the sponge well risen.

MACGREGOR'S ATHOLE BROSE

Roy MacGregor GP, TVam doctor

Guaranteed to stiffen the arteries and satisfy stomachs. This comes with a warning that it is of absolutely no health benefit whatsoever, but is truly delicious.

double cream (go for that really thick version that Marks & Spencer do)
honey (preferably the opaque heather honey made from Scottish lavender pollen)
whisky (blended will do but malt is even better. However, avoid the iodine-rich Islay malts, a good Spey malt is ideal)
pinhead oatmeal (this is a particular hard tiny droplet form of oatmeal not always easily found. It is hard and crunchy. If unavailable, a few flakes of ordinary oatmeal, used dry, can be substituted.)
sponge fingers (the ones that come in a packet, smooth on one side and gritty on the other)

A clean glass of the best whisky should be to hand for the cook at all times throughout preparation. This is essential if the rich taste is to be cleared between each tasting as the right consistency is sought.

Take $\frac{1}{2}$ pint/250 ml of double cream and whip.

To a small bowl add 2 dessertspoons/20 ml of heather honey.

Pour into a measure 3 dessertspoons/30 ml of whisky.

Add 4 dessertspoons/40 ml of whipped cream to the heather honey. Do not mix. Pour whisky around the edge of the bowl covering all surfaces if possible.

Fold gently the cream, honey and whisky together.

The final consistency should be that of a stiff dip. If too runny, add further honey. Portion size variable. Use remaining cream to make further portions. Advisable not to attempt larger quantities at one go than above for fear of wasting whisky.

Store each portion already served into glasses, or small dessert dishes, for at least 1 hour in the fridge.

Serving: Add the pinhead oatmeal at the last minute sprinkled thinly on top. Serve direct from the fridge with two sponge fingers per person.

KATRINA'S APPLE CAKE

Lisa Appignanesi, writer

2 eggs
8 oz/225 g sugar
1 teaspoon/5 ml vanilla
4 fl oz/100 ml oil
3 tablespoons/45 ml water or juice
12 oz/350 g flour

2 teaspoons/10 ml baking powder
¼ teaspoon/1 ml salt
6–8 apples, thinly sliced
4 oz/125 g white or brown sugar
2 teaspoons/10 ml cinnamon
sprinkled icing sugar

Beat eggs, sugar and vanilla until fluffy. Beat in oil. Add liquid alternately with dry ingredients and beat until just smooth. Spoon half of the batter into lightly greased 9″(23 cm) pan. Spread evenly. Add apples which have been sprinkled with sugar and cinnamon. Cover with remaining batter. Bake at 350F/180C/ gas mark 4 for 50–60 minutes until nicely browned. Increase proportions by a third for larger cake.

Equally delicious with cherries or plums or blackberries.

BANANA FOOL

Alex Forshaw, Islington's Conservation Officer

Serves 6

Mash or blend 4–5 ripe bananas with 1 pint/500 ml of crème fraîche or plain yoghurt. Mix in brown muscavado sugar to taste and a slosh or two of Armagnac, Cognac or any of those interesting half-empty bottles you've had stored away for ages. Bananas will go with almost anything! A solid biscuit base is an optional extra, made from melted butter and crumbled digestive biscuits, pressed into a flan dish. Alternatively pour the fool into small individual bowls and sprinkle with dark grated chocolate.

I've always liked mashed bananas, so here's a good use for them when they get a bit squidgy, and a pleasant way to increase your potassium intake.

FLO'S DELICIOUS 'AFTER THE SHOW' BREAD PUDDING

Flo Jeffries and all, The Little Angel Marionette Theatre, Dagmar Passage

1 lb/450 g stale bread
4 oz/125 g currants/raisins
5 oz/150 g sugar
1 oz/25 g mixed spice

½ teaspoon/2.5 ml nutmeg
2 large eggs
8 oz/225 g butter or margarine

Soak bread in cold water for 1 hour. Squeeze out as much moisture as possible and break up bread with a fork. Mix in: fruit, sugar, spice, nutmeg, eggs, and melted fat. Put mixture in well-greased tin. Bake for 1 hour (approx.) in pre-heated oven, 350F/180C/gas mark 4.

MULBERRY MOUSSE Fiona Boyle, administrator, the Tower Theatre

This recipe is inspired by the ancient mulberry tree in the garden of Canonbury Tower – our headquarters – built in the 16th century.

12 oz/350 g mulberries
1 tablespoon/15 ml water
2 eggs
1 egg yolk
3 oz/75 g caster sugar
½ oz/15 g gelatine, soaked in 3 tablespoons/45 ml cold water
10 fl oz/280g double cream, or imitation cream, lightly whipped.

Set aside a few mulberries. Place the rest in a pan with the water and simmer gently for 5 minutes. Cool slightly, then pour into the blender. Blend on maximum speed for 30 seconds. Sieve to remove pips.

Place the eggs, egg yolk and sugar in the mixing bowl and whisk on high speed for 5 minutes until thick.

Heat gelatine gently until dissolved, then fold in the egg mousse with the mulberries and half the cream.

Turn into a 2 pint/1.2 litre glass dish and chill until set. Whip the remaining cream until stiff. Decorate the mousse with piped cream and mulberries.

If you cannot get mulberries, this recipe works just as well with blackberries or raspberries.

BANANA SOYA DESSERT

Chuka and Dubem Okonkwo, The Highbury Twins

2 oz/50 g soya beans
4–5 large ripe bananas
strip of Khombu*

Soak beans overnight. Cook the following day with a strip of Khombu that has been soaked for 1 hour. Make sure that the beans are very well cooked and that the Khombu is soft. Once the beans are ready, remove from the Khombu and blend with the bananas. This is delicious on its own or served with cake.

*Khombu is a green sea vegetable, full of minerals and extremely tough to cook. A strip is used at a time, soaking it in a pot of water before cooking with beans. It helps to make beans digestible, and the beans soften the sea vegetable.

CREME BRULEE

Linda Gumb, antique dealer, Camden Passage

6 egg yolks
4 oz/100 g caster sugar
$\frac{1}{2}$ pint/250 ml double cream
$\frac{1}{2}$ pint/250 ml single cream
Demerara sugar

Crack egg yolks into a basin. With a wooden spoon add the sugar to the egg yolks and beat thoroughly. Put the cream into a saucepan and almost bring to the boil, then pour slowly over the yolks, stirring well.

Strain the custard into a fireproof dish. Place in a shallow baking tin with 1"(2.5 cm) of cold water up the sides of the dish. Put into a slow oven, 300F/150C/gas mark 2, and bake for 1–1$\frac{1}{2}$ hours until the custard is firmly set. Remove from heat and allow to cool, then put in fridge.

One hour before serving, sprinkle the top with Demerara sugar covering the whole surface. Brown under a very hot grill. Allow to cool and the top will become hard. Can be served with cream.

SOUR CREAM CAKE

Susan Barrie, hairdresser

1 small packet digestive biscuits
2 oz/50 g melted butter
$\frac{1}{2}$ teaspoon/2.5 ml cinnamon
4 small cartons sour cream
1 small tin mandarins
1 cup caster sugar

Crush biscuits, add cinnamon and melted butter and press into the bottom of a 7″(18 cm) spring form tin. Drain mandarins, put a few aside for decoration, and mix remaining with sour cream and sugar. Pour into tin. Put rest of mandarins on top. Bake in oven 350F/180C/gas mark 4 for 20 minutes. Let it get very cold before removing from tin.

BAKED FUDGE PUDDING

Dennis Marret, barber, Huckers

1. 1 cup flour
   $\frac{1}{2}$ cup sugar
   2 tablespoons/30 ml cocoa
   2 teaspoons/10 ml baking powder
   $\frac{1}{2}$ teaspoon/2.5 ml salt
   $\frac{1}{2}$ cup milk
   2 tablespoons/30 ml melted butter
   $\frac{1}{2}$ teaspoon/2.5 ml vanilla essence

2. $\frac{3}{4}$ cup brown sugar
   $\frac{1}{4}$ cup cocoa

3. $\frac{3}{4}$ cups boiling water

Mix dry ingredients in 1. together. Add wet ingredients from 1. to make a sticky base and spoon into a greased, ovenproof glass bowl. Mix ingredients in 2. together and pour over the top of base mixture. Finally pour water in 3. over the top of the whole mixture in bowl.

Bake at 350F/180C/gas mark 4 for 40 minutes.

Option: add chopped nuts to base 1. mixture.

Wonderful hot or cold.

DUTCH APPLE PIE (APPLETAART)

Marianne Fox Ockinga, artist

8 oz/250 g flour	pinch of salt
6 oz/175 g margarine	10 hard apples
4 oz/100 g sugar	grated lemon rind
1 egg	sugar to taste

Make the first five ingredients into a dough, roll out and line a greased 10″(26 cm) cake tin. Cut 10 hard apples into pieces, using different varieties. Add grated lemon rind and sugar to taste. Cut up the rest of the dough into strips and make a lattice pattern over the top. Put in oven at 400F/200C/gas mark 6 for about $\frac{1}{2}$ hour, then turn oven down and leave for another $\frac{1}{2}$ hour or longer. Use foil underneath to catch the juices.

MAUD'S CHOCOLATE PUDDING

Canonbury Bookshop

6 oz/175 g plain chocolate
4 oz/125 g butter
2 oz/50 g caster sugar
2 eggs, separated
1 packet sponge cakes

Melt the chocolate in a small quantity of hot water and allow to cool.

Beat butter and sugar to a cream, add egg yolks and beat again.

Add melted chocolate and beat for 10 minutes.

Beat egg whites until stiff and stir into mixture.

Melt a little sugar in tepid water (add 1 tablespoon/15 ml rum – optional).

Cut sponge cakes in half (longways) and soak in sugar mixture.

Arrange pieces in 6″(15 cm) cake tin (sides and bottom), leave some for top.

Pour in chocolate mixture, and cover with remaining sponge cakes.

Cover with small plate with weight and let stand all night in fridge.

LEMON CHEESECAKE

Allan's Shoe Shop, Upper Street, Islington
Has been fitting shoes to the residents of Islington since 1869.

Serves 8

2 oz/50 g butter/margarine
2 oz/50 g caster sugar
4 oz/125 g digestive biscuits (8 biscuits)

Biscuit Base:
Melt butter and sugar over low heat, add crushed biscuits. Press into base of
loose-bottomed tin. Chill in fridge.

Top:
8 oz/225 g curd cheese, or soft cream cheese
2 eggs, separated
4 oz/125 g caster sugar
grated rind of 2 lemons
$\frac{1}{4}$ pint/150 ml double cream (or whipping cream)
juice of 2 lemons
2 tablespoons/30 ml water
$\frac{1}{2}$ oz/12 g gelatine

Soften cheese in large bowl. Beat in egg yolks, 2 oz/50 g sugar, lemon rind
and cream.

Put lemon juice, water and gelatine in small heat-proof bowl over saucepan
of hot water until gelatine is dissolved. Beat into cheese mixture. Leave until
on point of setting. Whisk egg whites until stiff. Whisk in 2 oz/50 g sugar.

Fold into mixture. Spoon into prepared tin.

Chill for 3–4 hours. Run a knife gently round the tin and remove.

Decorate with grated chocolate.

AN ABUNDANCE OF APRICOTS

Mary Kleinman, artist

Poach 2 packets of apricots and when cool add 2 tablespoons/30 ml of brandy. Leave for an hour or so (covered). Heap onto a large white or blue plate. Sprinkle with lots of toasted almond flakes, garnish with 2 or 3 scented geranium leaves, and serve with a jug of thin cream or a heap of Greek yoghurt and a dish of macaroons.

INDIAN PUDDING

Ann Usborne, artist

This recipe is from *Fannie Farmer's Boston Cooking School Cookbook*, first published 1896.

Serves 6–8

Corn meal cooked very slowly with milk, molasses, and spice is the classic New England Indian Pudding. It should be soft and should separate somewhat. It is important to use the best dark molasses (or black treacle) for the finest flavour. Let a true Indian Pudding stand for half an hour after baking so that it will be slightly firmer.

Heat in a heavy saucepan

   2 cups of milk

Mix until smooth
   $\frac{1}{4}$ cup yellow corn meal
   $\frac{1}{4}$ cup cold milk

Stir into the hot milk. Cook over hot water for 20 minutes, stirring frequently. Add

   $\frac{1}{2}$ cup dark molasses
   1 teaspoon/5 ml salt
   $\frac{1}{4}$ cup sugar
   1 teaspoon/5 ml each cinnamon and ground ginger
   $\frac{1}{4}$ cup butter

Stir and pour into a buttered pudding dish.

Pour over the top

   $1\frac{3}{4}$ cups cold milk

Bake for 1 hour at 350F/180C/gas mark 4.

Serve with heavy cream or vanilla ice cream.

PUFF PASTRY YUM YUM

Annie Williams, artist

7 oz/200 g frozen puff pastry
3 oz/75 g icing sugar
3 oz/75 g butter

3 oz/75 g ground almonds
1 egg yolk
rum

Roll out the pastry into two circles and place one on the bottom of the baking dish. Cream butter, add most of the icing sugar, then almonds and egg yolk (and rum), and spread on pastry base. Seal on lid and put in oven at 400F/200C/gas mark 6 for 10 minutes. Take out of oven, place the second circle on top and brush with milk or egg and sprinkle with the remaining icing sugar.

Bake in oven at 450F/230C/gas mark 8 for 5–10 minutes.

Serve hot with cream.

MINT ICE CREAM AND MINT SAUCE (Yes – together!)

Jennifer Vernor-Miles, NSPCC Committee

Pick 4 handfuls of mint leaves stripped from stem. Wash, and put in blender with juice of 4 lemons.

Bring to boil 1 pint/500 ml water, in which is dissolved 1 lb/450 g caster sugar. Cool a little, then pour syrup onto mint leaves and blend. Strain into a suitable container for freezing, pressing as much juice as possible through the sieve. Cool, then freeze.

Meanwhile, take the mint leaves from the strainer, half fill a jam-jar and fill up to the top with wine vinegar. Put lid on securely, and shake vigorously. Test consistency (it may need more vinegar; the leaves must be covered). This will keep for months and, although it will lose some colour, the taste remains.

Back to the ice cream … Whip 1 pint/500 ml double cream but not to absolute stiffness. Cut frozen syrup out in lumps and return to the blender. Whizz until it is all sorbet-looking and mushy. Then deftly and quickly stir it into the whipped cream (if you are slow about this the cold syrup freezes the cream into lumps, so the ice cream isn't smooth). Don't worry if it looks a bit liquid at this stage. Pour into freezer containers and freeze.

PEACH MOUSSE

The Continental Touch, Spanish delicatessen

1 tin of peaches in syrup
3 eggs
1 lemon
6 tablespoons/90 ml condensed milk

Drain peaches and make a purée with them. Mix the 3 egg yolks with lemon juice, condensed milk and peach purée. Beat egg whites until stiff and fold gently into mixture. Chill well. Decorate with bits of peach.

PASSION CAKE

Gill Wing, Le Café

$\frac{1}{2}$ pint/250 ml sunflower oil
12 oz/350 g soft brown sugar
2 teaspoons/10 ml vanilla
4 size 3 eggs (or 2 size 2)

Put all ingredients together in blender and blend to a thick cream.

15 oz/400 g can crushed pineapple	3 oz/75 g coconut
12 oz/350 g grated carrot	4 oz/125 g nuts

Stir into cream mixture.

8 oz/225 g plain wholemeal flour	2 teaspoon/10 ml bicarbonate of soda
1 teaspoon/5 ml salt	3 teaspoon/15 ml cinnamon
1 teaspoon/5 ml baking powder	

Fold into mixture quite runny.
Bake at 350F/180C/gas mark 4 for $1\frac{3}{4}$ hours using large meat tin.

Icing:
8 oz/225 g icing sugar
4 oz/125 g margarine
4 oz/125 g Philadelphia cheese

Blend together, keeping quite runny and pour over cake.

APPLE AND MINCEMEAT STEAM PUDDING

The Albion Pub

4 oz/125 g butter, softened
4 oz/125 g caster sugar
5 oz/150 g self-raising flour
pinch of salt
grated zest of 1½ lemon
2 eggs, size 1
1 medium-size Bramley apple, unpeeled and roughly chopped
3 heaped tablespoons/50 ml mincemeat

Put butter, sugar, flour, salt and lemon in bowl. Break in the eggs and beat for about 4 minutes until creamy. Fold in apple chunks. Put the mincemeat in the bottom of a 1½ pint/750 ml well-buttered pudding basin. Put mixture on top. Cover with foil (put a pleat in to allow for expansion) and steam for 2½ hours.

Do not boil dry.

Delicious.

LEMON DELICIOUS

Granita's Restaurant

1 large tablespoon/15 ml butter
1 cup sugar
1 tablespoon/15 ml flour
juice of 1 large lemon
2 eggs
1 cup milk

Cream butter and sugar, add flour and lemon juice. Add egg yolks and a cup of milk. Beat egg whites until stiff and fold into mixture. Pour into a heatproof dish (the mixture should sit at least 6″ (15 cm) deep). Sit in water bath for 45–60 minutes in medium oven, 350F/180C/gas mark 4. It is ready when lightly browned on top. It should be foamy on top and almost liquid at the bottom.

Serve with fresh or poached fruit, cookies or lots of whipped cream.

MOTHER'S CHRISTMAS PUDDING

Diana Matthews, estate agent

8 oz/225 g raisins
2 oz/50 g candied peel
8 oz/225 g currants
8 oz/225 g sultanas
3 tablespoons/45 ml rum
8 oz/225 g butter
grated rind 1 orange and 1 lemon
8 oz/225 g soft brown sugar
4 eggs
4 oz/125 g plain flour
$\frac{1}{2}$ teaspoon/2.5 ml salt
4 oz/125 g fresh breadcrumbs
mixed spice, grated nutmeg, ground ginger, ground cinnamon and
   bicarbonate of soda.

Chop raisins and candied peel and, together with currants and sultanas,
sprinkle with rum and leave overnight.

Next day: cream butter, sugar and add fruit rinds. Add beaten eggs gradually,
beating well. Stir in fruit alternately with sifted flour, spices, salt and
breadcrumbs.

Line large well-buttered pudding basin with circle of greased grease-proof
paper cut to fit the base. Put pudding into basin and cover with another circle
of grease-proof paper to fit over the top of pudding basin. Cover and tie with
a scalded muslin cloth.

Steam in saucepan of boiling water, covered, for 6 hours. Water should come
halfway up the basin. Keep topped up. When cold, cover with fresh grease-
proof paper and tie with string.

To serve: put pudding into saucepan of boiling water and steam for $2\frac{1}{2}$ hours.

CRUNCHIE BAR ICE CREAM

Greg Coad, Manager, Islington Majestic Wine Warehouse

An easy recipe for ice cream, that tastes fantastic, and needs *no stirring* whilst it freezes.

1 pint/500 ml double cream, or whipping cream, chilled
half a large can/400 g condensed milk
pinch of salt
1 tablespoon/15 ml Gold Blend type instant coffee
1½ tablespoons/20 ml brandy
1 Crunchie bar

Mix/whip together the cream, condensed milk and salt, and refrigerate for 1 hour. Beat until peaks form (this is best done in a Kenwood Chefette). Then add the coffee dissolved in the brandy, and the Crunchie bar roughly crushed (done in a plastic bag with a rolling pin). You can at this stage, if wanted, fold in some melted good quality dark cooking chocolate to create a rippled effect. Then simply freeze for at least 3 hours, transferring to fridge for 30 minutes prior to serving.

The amount of coffee, Crunchie bar and chocolate can be adjusted to suit individual tastes.

TARTE TATIN

Gerald Harper, actor

| puff pastry | brown sugar |
| butter | cooking apples |

Take a round 7" (18 cm) baking tin. Smear liberally with several ounces of butter and then cover with a thick layer of any brown sugar. Fill with peeled sliced apples. Put over heat until butter and sugar bubble nicely and start to caramelize. Cover with a round of puff pastry and bake in a hot oven, 400F/200C/gas mark 6, until pastry is done. Then cover with a large plate, hold your breath and turn upside down. Out pops the tarte to gasps all round.

It never fails and you don't need to measure.

FRUITS BRULES

Nigel Slater, cookery writer

Serves 6

A recipe from my book, *Real Fast Puddings*.

This summer pudding really excels when it is made with soft fruits, berries (black-, blue- and raspberries), peaches, if they are really ripe, and bananas. Redcurrants look like glistening jewels if a sprig or two is laid on top of the peaks of cream.

8 oz/225 g sugar
1 ½ lb/700 g mixed soft fruits, to include raspberries, bananas and peaches
12 fl oz/350 ml double cream, chilled

Put the sugar in a heavy pan and pour in enough water to cover. Set over a high flame to boil, while you prepare the fruit. Peel the bananas, stone and slice the peaches and rinse the raspberries. Put all the fruit in a heat-proof serving bowl. Whip the cream until it is stiff and spoon over the fruit so that it stands up in peaks.

The sugar in the pan will start to turn to a pale golden caramel after about 10 minutes, maybe less. Watch it carefully as it is prone to burning, but do not stir it. The caramel is ready when it turns a rich golden brown. Take it off the heat before it starts to smoke or it will turn bitter.

Immediately, taking care not to burn yourself, pour the caramel over the cream and fruit. It will set at once to a crisp, shiny coat.

Islington was originally a dairy farming community, so it is good to see that the area still has two wonderful cheese shops. Elliot's Butchers, on Essex Road, has a counter packed with British cheeses, all made by hand in small dairies. In Highbury, there is now La Fromagerie, a tiny shop packed with French and Italian varieties, not to mention good bread and croissants. My recipes are based on cheese and cream.

BANANA FLAMBE

The Gibsons' favourite pudding.

David Gibson, architect

1 banana per person, cut lengthways
1 level dessertspoon/10 ml soft brown sugar per banana
1 oz/25 g butter for each banana
sprinkling of lemon juice

Put all the banana halves into a frying pan with the butter and sugar. As the butter and sugar melt, spoon them over the bananas. Cook for 2–3 minutes. Serve. This is nice with brandy or rum, added at the end, and served with whipped cream.

FRUIT CLAFOUTIS

Muriel Feder, NSPCC Committee

14 oz/400 g tin of pitted cherries	2 oz/50 g flour
8 oz/225 g tin of apricots	$\frac{1}{2}$ pint/300 ml milk
3 eggs	$\frac{1}{4}$ pint/150 ml double cream
4 oz/125 g caster sugar	icing sugar to serve

Heat the oven to 375F/150C/gas mark 5.

Drain the cherries and apricots and place them in an oven-proof dish.

Whisk the eggs and caster sugar in a bowl until light and fluffy, then sift in the flour and whisk again until the mixture is smooth.

Gradually whisk in the milk and cream. Pour this batter over the fruit and cook in the pre-heated oven for 45 minutes or until it is just set and the top is golden brown. You can serve immediately or keep it warm in a low oven until ready to serve. Immediately before serving, sprinkle the top with sieved icing sugar.

It is also delicious cold.

You can use any fruit, tinned or fresh, for this pud.

BREAD AND BUTTER PUDDING

Katharine Hamnett, fashion designer

For people who like their bread buttered.

1 pint/500 ml milk
1 egg
1 dessertspoon/10 ml caster sugar
4 slices white bread (buttered on both sides and cut into four)
1½ handfuls currants (thoroughly washed)
1½ teaspoons/7.5 ml tangerine rind, finely cut

Beat egg and sugar together, then slowly add milk. Pour mixture into a round 9″ (23 cm) ovenproof dish. Add currants and tangerine rind. Float bread pieces on top. Bake in hot oven, 400F/200C/gas mark 6, for 25 minutes, or until top is golden brown.

Marian Fox Ockinga

PORRIDGE	160	Mr Barber, caterer, HM Prison, Pentonville
MORNING BREAKFAST JUICES	160	Chuka and Dubem Okonkwo, The Highbury Twins
AUBERGINE PIE	161	Jenny Blanchard, designer
FESTIVE FILO PIE WITH WATERCRESS SAUCE	162	Stephen Remington, Director, Sadlers Wells
SWEET AND SPICY MUSHROOMS	163	Ruth Thomson, children's writer
COURGETTE PIE	164	Rena Salaman, cookery writer
PIMIENTOS A LA MALAGENA	165	The Finca, Tapas Bar and Restaurant, Pentonville Road
POTATO CHEESE (HIMALAYAN STYLE)	165	Deborah Dorjee, Hair at Canonbury Place
THE WORKING WOMAN'S NO-TIME, LOW-COST, LOW-CHOLESTROL, HAPPY, HEALTHY GASTRONOMIC DAY PORRIDGE AND HUMOUS	166	Elspeth Morley, British Assoc. of Psychotherapists

VEGETARIAN

SERENDIPITOUS PARSNIP AND APPLE	167	Nina Bawden, author
GOLDEN VEGETABLE LAYER	168	Waterside Inn, York Way
SPANAKOPITA	168	Alec Forshaw, Islington's Conservation Officer
PILAW RICE	169	Mrs K Mehta, Lovely Looks Eastern Boutique
VEGETABLE LASAGNE	170	John Melvin, architect
LEEK AND DUMPLING CASSEROLE	172	Isobel Buchanan, opera singer
POTATO PUDDING	173	Susan Barrie, hairdresser
TABBOULEH	173	Anne-Sophie Wade, NSPCC Committee
FLAN DE POIVRONS	174	Patrick Milmo, QC
CORN PUDDING	175	Richard Wentworth, sculptor

PORRIDGE

Mr Barber, Caterer, HM Prison Pentonville

Porridge is still served in prisons and indeed prison folklore has it that on the day of discharge a prisoner must eat his porridge otherwise he will return to eat it at a later date!

4 oz/110 g rolled oats
2 pints/1.2 litre water
pinch of salt
1 oz/25 g sugar (optional)
½ pint/300 ml milk

Bring the water to the boil. Stir in the rolled oats, bring to the boil, stirring frequently. Add salt and sugar, if required, and allow to simmer gently for 10–15 minutes.

Serve with hot milk.

MORNING BREAKFAST JUICES

Chuka and Dubem Okonkwo, The Highbury Twins

3 apples
3 celery sticks
1 piece ginger root

or

2 beetroots
3 apples
2 celery sticks
4 kiwis
1 piece ginger root

or

3 apples
2 carrots
1 piece ginger root

Wash thoroughly and squeeze through a juice extractor.

AUBERGINE PIE

Jenny Blanchard, designer

The source of this recipe is Jocasta Innes.

Serves 6–8

1 lb/450 g aubergines, sliced
salt and pepper
3 tablespoons/45 ml oil
8 oz/250 g Mozzarella cheese, sliced
1 tablespoon/15 ml grated Parmesan cheese
2 tablespoons/30 ml breadcrumbs

Tomato sauce:
1 tablespoon/15 ml oil
1 clove garlic, crushed
1 large onion, chopped
1 lb/450 g tomatoes, skinned, seeded and chopped
1 bouquet garni
3 tablespoons/45 ml dry white wine
1 teaspoon/5 ml Worcester sauce
1 tablespoon/15 ml tomato purée

Sprinkle the aubergines with salt, place in a colander and leave for 1 hour. Rinse in cold water and dry on kitchen paper.

Meanwhile, make the sauce. Heat the oil in a pan, add the garlic and onion and sauté until soft. Add the tomatoes and cook for 2 minutes. Add the remaining ingredients, with salt and pepper to taste. Simmer uncovered for 45 minutes, until thickened. Remove bouquet garni.

Heat the oil in a frying pan, add the aubergine slices and fry until golden. Drain on kitchen paper.

Fill a shallow ovenproof dish with alternate layers of aubergines, Mozzarella and tomato sauce, finishing with cheese. Sprinkle with Parmesan and breadcrumbs.

Bake in a preheated moderately hot oven, 400F/200C/gas mark 6, for 30 minutes. Serve hot or cold.

FESTIVE FILO PIE

Stephen Remington, Director, Sadlers Wells

5 tablespoons/75 ml olive oil
1 onion, thinly chopped
3 sticks celery, sliced
2 garlic cloves, crushed
1 lb/450 g button mushrooms
1 medium apple, cored and sliced
2 tablespoons/30 ml fresh parsley,
    chopped

1 tablespoon/15 ml caraway seeds
2 tablespoons/30 ml dry sherry
4 oz/125 g cream cheese
2 eggs, beaten
2 oz/50 g butter
8–10 sheets filo pastry, thawed
salt and pepper

Pre-heat oven to 400F/200C/gas mark 6.

Heat 3 tablespoons/45 ml of the olive oil in a large saucepan and fry onions
gently for approximately 5 minutes, until softened not browned. Add celery
and garlic and cook for further 4 minutes, stirring occasionally. Next add
mushrooms, apple, parsley and caraway seeds and cook for 5 minutes stirring
frequently. Add sherry and seasoning and cook for further 5 minutes. Then put
the pan on the side to cool.

In a separate bowl combine cream cheese and eggs. Drain the mushroom
mixture, reserving the liquid for the sauce, and combine with the eggs and
cheese.

Grease a shallow 2½ pint/1.50 litre ovenproof dish. Heat butter and remaining
oil.

Unfold filo pastry and line dish with 2–3 sheets, brushing pastry with melted
butter/olive oil. Spoon the mixture into the dish and cover with remaining
pastry sheets, brushing the layers with melted butter. This will prevent the
layers from sticking together. Cook for 40–45 minutes until the pie has risen
and is crispy and golden.

Serve with *Watercress Sauce*.

WATERCRESS SAUCE

6 oz/175 g watercress, washed
1½ oz/35 g butter
½ pint/300 ml vegetable stock, including
    liquid from the mushrooms

½ oz/12 g wholemeal flour
½ pint/300 ml single cream
seasoning

Trim watercress and blanch in boiling water for 2 minutes until softened.

Drain, rinse and drain again. Then finely chop.

In a small pan, heat the butter and watercress and cook for 2 minutes. Stir in the flour and cook for 1 minute, then add the stock gradually, stirring continuously. Bring the sauce up to the boil and simmer for 3 minutes. Season to taste. Leave to cool and stir in the cream. Reheat very gently just before serving.

SWEET AND SPICY MUSHROOMS

Ruth Thomson, children's writer

This rich dish is an ideal winter starter served with brown toast, or provides a perfect foil for bland foods, such as baked potatoes.

1 large onion
4 oz/125 g butter
2 red peppers
1 lb/450 g button mushrooms

Sauce:
2 tablespoons/30 ml Dijon mustard
4 oz/125 g dark brown sugar
2 tablespoons/30 ml Worcester sauce
1 cup red wine or grape juice
black pepper and salt

Peel and chop the onion. Sauté it in butter in a large saucepan. Cut the peppers into small chunks. Cut the mushrooms in half.

While you wait for the onion to become transparent, prepare the sauce.

Mix the mustard, sugar and Worcester sauce together to make a paste. Stir in the wine or juice and add pepper and salt to taste.

When the onion is clear, stir in the mushrooms and peppers. Sauté until the mushrooms turn brown, stirring all the time. Then mix in the sauce. Simmer the mushrooms without a lid for 40–60 minutes, until the sauce has thickened.

COURGETTE PIE (KOLOKYTHOPITTA)

Rena Salaman, cookery writer

Serves 6–8

Vegetable pies are a great tradition in Greece, often using homemade rustic pastry. However, for more decorous instances the paper-thin sheets of filo pastry are used, bought ready-made. Filo was introduced into this country by Greek Cypriots in the early Fifties and has become so popular that it is now stocked by all major supermarkets and used by chefs at fashionable restaurants for dainty creations with savoury or sweet fillings.

This pie is a variation of one made on the Ionian island of Corfu. It is purely vegetarian, light and delicious.

1¼lb/575 g courgettes, trimmed, rinsed and dried
4 eggs, lightly beaten
2–3 spring onions, trimmed, rinsed and sliced finely
4 oz/125 g feta cheese, crumbled
3 tablespoons/45 ml fresh dill, chopped
salt and black pepper
14 oz/400 g packet filo pastry
4 oz/125 g melted butter

Pre-heat oven to 375F/190C/gas mark 5.

Coarsely grate courgettes through a food processor. Beat eggs lightly in a large bowl and add remaining filling ingredients including courgettes. Mix well.

Oil the base and sides of a medium-size roasting dish and line its base with a sheet of pastry that has first been brushed with butter. Continue in the same fashion, first brushing each sheet with butter until about half the pastry has been used, placing each sheet as accurately as you can. Spread the filling evenly and neatly fold all pastry sides over it. Cover with remaining pastry, first brushing each sheet with butter. Butter top sheet liberally. Trim excess edges all round or tack them in at the sides.

Using a sharp knife, cut the top layers of pastry only (otherwise the filling might spill), into squares or lozenge pieces, approximately 3″ × 2½″ (8 cm × 5 cm). Sprinkle over a little cold water with the tips of your fingers to prevent the pastry edges curling up.

Bake in oven for 45 minutes, until crisp and light golden. Take out and let stand for at least 5 minutes before serving. For best results serve hot or warm, but it can also be served at room temperature.

PIMIENTOS A LA MALAGENA (PEPPERS MALAGA STYLE)

The Finca, Tapas Bar and Restaurant, Pentonville Road

3 red peppers	1 onion	$\frac{1}{2}$ cup olive oil
3 green peppers	$\frac{1}{2}$ cup raisins	salt and pepper

You will need a casserole dish with a lid.

To prepare peppers, cut in half, remove seeds and slice lengthways into strips. Slice onion thickly. Place peppers, onions and all other ingredients in casserole. Stir so that everything is mixed together and put in hot oven, 400F/200C/gas mark 6, for 30 minutes, stirring once or twice. This dish can be eaten hot or cold. It is delicious served chilled with bread on a hot day.

POTATO CHEESE (HIMALAYAN STYLE)

Deborah Dorjee, Hair at Canonbury Place

6 medium sized potatoes
2 green peppers
1 small green chilli
1 large clove garlic
$\frac{1}{2}$ oz/15 g butter
4 oz/100 g grated mature Cheddar cheese (or yak cheese, if available)

Peel the potatoes and slice thickly. Cut green peppers into strips. Chop the green chilli and garlic finely and put into cooking pot with enough water to just cover ingredients. Add butter and $\frac{1}{2}$ teaspoon/2.5 ml salt and bring to the boil. Add grated cheeses just before potatoes are cooked and simmer until they are fully cooked. Stir gently once cooked.

Serve with rice.

THE WORKING WOMAN'S NO-TIME, LOW-COST, LOW-CHOLESTROL, HAPPY, HEALTHY GASTRONOMIC DAY

Elspeth Morley, British Association of Psychotherapists

You work hard all day. You cook a substantial meal for yourself and others in the evening. You want to eat on your own during the day, enjoyably and healthily if repetitiously, and above all swiftly. You have no time or inclination for further cooking, or even further thought.

Why not start with a daily bowl of porridge, made substantially from oatbran, that miraculous soluble fibre which absorbs fourteen times its weight in liquid, so leaves you feeling full out of all proportion to its low calorific content? Cooked once in 5 days, it can be kept in 5 individual bowls in the fridge, ready for 2 minutes heating in the microwave each morning.

PORRIDGE:

$\frac{3}{4}$ cup rolled oats
$\frac{1}{2}$ cup oatbran (obtainable from health food shops or Sainsburys)
2 tablespoons/30 ml skimmed milk powder
5 cups cold water
1 teaspoon/5 ml salt
maple syrup or brown sugar and milk to serve

Bring porridge slowly to boil, stirring constantly, and simmer for 5 minutes before dividing into serving bowls.

Launched by porridge into a morning of warm inner contentment, you are ready for a light spicy lunch of minimal preparation and effort. For this I recommend a cup of broth, with home-made humous on wholemeal toast, or on the delicious Greek olive bread to be found in most delicatessens. A broth made every 5 days from simmering together any combination of the wilting outside leaves etc. of any vegetables and perhaps the dregs of any wine bottles, is good as it comes. But if you are using a commercial broth, even the best Swiss bouillons, the flavour is much enhanced by the addition of 2 tablespoons/30 ml of Sainsbury's Clamato, a delicious tomato and clams cocktail, as its name implies.

HUMOUS:

8 oz/225 g split peas
4 cloves garlic
1 chilli, fresh or dried
2 tablespoons/30 ml Tahini (sesame seed concentrate, from health food shops)
stock cube, the Chinese or Mexican Oxo cubes are an exciting variation
juice of 1 lemon
1 tablespoon/15 ml olive oil

Soak the split peas for some hours, rinse and cover with water to 2″(5 cm) above the peas. Add the chilli and 2 of the garlic cloves and simmer until soft. Mix, either by hand, or with an electric blender if you prefer a smoother texture, with the Tahini, remaining garlic, stock cube and lemon juice, adding olive oil if necessary. The humous will store for up to 5 days in the fridge, and also freezes well.

This should see you through happily until supper, for which all more time-consuming, less healthy extravagances should be reserved for shared conviviality. But should you be tempted to snack en route, keep in readiness a store of Jordans muesli bars, made to the original oatbran recipe, which will again absorb an accompanying drink in a satisfying way. Or home-made marmalade, made once a year in January with Seville oranges and brown sugar, spooned onto oatcakes, will make a snack to bear daily repetition until next Christmas.

SERENDIPITOUS PARSNIP AND APPLE   Nina Bawden, author

It is the men in my family who cook the main dishes. My task, and my interest, is soup. There is an excellent parsnip and apple soup to be made with several parsnips and sweet apples and very good chicken stock. Simmer until the parsnips are soft, then put in a whizz machine or push through a sieve.

This recipe, however, I hit upon by sheer luck... and forgetfulness. I had put my soup on and gone to my desk and it was not until almost too late that I retrieved it. Too late, alas, for soup; but not too late for the most delicious alternative to mashed potatoes I know. Stewed parsnips and apples, cooked together in really good, jellified chicken stock until all the liquid has gone, and then beaten to the consistency of smooth mashed potatoes, are good with poultry, wonderful with game and venison, and, indeed, very edible on their own.

GOLDEN VEGETABLE LAYER

Waterside Inn, York Way

1 swede, peeled	1–2 cloves garlic, peeled
1 turnip, peeled	1 tablespoon/15 ml oil
1 parsnip, peeled	$\frac{1}{2}$ pint/250 ml water
2 medium carrots, peeled	2 tablespoons/30 ml tomato purée
2 onions, peeled	1 teaspoon/5 ml oregano
10 oz/275 g Cheddar cheese, grated	salt and pepper to taste
12 oz/350 g tomatoes	

The layer:
Shred the swede, turnip, parsnip, carrots and one of the onions.
Place half the amount of the shredded vegetables into a casserole dish, then half the cheese, then the second half of the vegetables, and top it with the rest of the cheese.

Season to taste.

The sauce:
Chop the tomatoes, garlic and the second onion.

Fry onion in oil until soft, add garlic, tomatoes, water, tomato purée and oregano.

Simmer for 20 minutes.

Place the sauce on top of the vegetable layer and bake in oven for 30 minutes at 350F/180C/gas mark 4.

SPANAKOPITA

Alec Forshaw, Islington's Conservation Officer

Serves 6

Islington is well-known for its large Cypriot population, and as a long-standing resident of Holloway I commend this dish as a tribute to the ready availability of the necessary ingredients. It is also a welcome main course for vegetarians which most carnivores enjoy too.

1 large (or 2 small) onions

olive oil

2 lbs/900 g defrosted frozen leaf spinach (or fresh spinach, washed and torn into shreds)

6 eggs, well-beaten

$\frac{1}{2}$ lb/225 g feta cheese, crumbled into small pieces

$\frac{1}{4}$ lb/110 g stoned black olives

2 teaspoon/10 ml oregano

ground black pepper

1 lb/450 g filo pastry (or strudel)

Chop the onion finely and sauté in olive oil for 5 minutes. When cool, tip these into a large mixing bowl and add the following: spinach, eggs, cheese, olives, oregano and pepper. Mix together thoroughly. Take a large oblong baking dish, smear inside with olive oil and line with filo pastry. A 1 lb/450 g pack of filo or strudel pastry should include about 20 sheets (I would not recommend trying to make it yourself; goodness knows how they get it so thin!). Use 15 sheets to line the bottom and sides, allowing plenty to hang over the edges. Pour in the contents of the mixing bowl and spread evenly. Use remaining 5 or so sheets to make a lid and fold in the overhanging sheets to make a neat and pretty seal. Cut three small slashes in the lid with a sharp knife. Brush top of the pastry with melted butter or olive oil. Bake at 400F/ 200C/gas mark 5 for 50 minutes.

Serve hot, cut into squares, with new potatoes and salad.

PILAW RICE   Mrs K Mehta, Lovely Looks Eastern Boutique

3 cups rice (Basmati)	3 cups mixed frozen vegetables
2 oz/50 g butter	$\frac{1}{4}$ teaspoon/1.5 ml saffron or turmeric
1 teaspoon/5 ml sesame seeds	20 cashew nuts
4 cloves	1 oz/25 g sultanas
3 small sticks cinnamon	$2\frac{1}{2}$ teaspoons/12.5 ml salt

Wash rice two to three times, rinse.

Put $1\frac{1}{2}$ oz/37 g butter into saucepan and add sesame seeds. When seeds start to pop add cloves, cinnamon and rice and fry until the rice is dry. Add vegetables, saffron (or tumeric), sultanas, nuts and salt. Add 9 cups of water and bring to the boil. Then simmer on low heat with lid on for 15 minutes. Add $\frac{1}{2}$ oz/12 g butter and simmer for another 5 minutes.

VEGETABLE LASAGNE John Melvin, architect

Serves 10 as a main course

Ratatouille:
1 lb/450 g onions, sliced
2 lbs/900 g courgettes, finely sliced
3 large aubergines
4 green peppers
2 tins chopped tomatoes
2 tablespoons/30 ml olive oil

2 packets 'no pre-cook' lasagne

1 packet grated mozzarella cheese

Bechamel sauce: (2 pints/1.25 litres)
4 oz/125 g margarine
4 oz/125 g flour
2 pints/1.25 litres milk
seasoning

METHOD:

Ratatouille:
Allow onions to sweat until soft in 2 tablespoons/30 ml olive oil.
Stir in the courgettes, and when these have cooked for about 4 minutes, add the aubergine, diced into small walnut-sized pieces. Then add the chopped tomatoes and sliced green peppers. Season to taste.

Simmer in a low oven, 325F/160C/gas mark 3, until cooked to a soft delicious goo.

Bechamel sauce:
Melt margarine on a low heat. Add flour until the mixture forms a soft ball, which is quite detached from the pan. Cook carefully for 1 minute. Slowly add the milk (this process is easier if the milk has been warmed). Stir constantly to eliminate all lumps, and then cook at boiling point for 30 seconds.

Line an open ovenproof dish with a layer of uncooked lasagne (my dishes are oval and very large); add a layer of half the ratatouille, topped by $\frac{1}{3}$ of the white sauce.

Then cover with a layer of uncooked lasagne, followed by the rest of the ratatouille and $\frac{1}{3}$ of the white sauce. One more layer of lasagne is topped with the remaining white sauce and covered thickly with grated mozzarella.

Bake in a medium oven, 400F/200C/gas mark 6, for 20–30 minutes until golden brown on top and sizzling.

JOHN MELVIN III 93.

John Melvin

LEEK AND DUMPLING CASSEROLE

Isobel Buchanan, opera singer

4 oz/125 g Aduki beans, soaked overnight
2 oz/50 g butter or margarine
1 onion, chopped
2 cloves garlic, crushed
1 lb/450 g leeks, trimmed and sliced
1 carrot, diced
8 oz/225 g mushrooms, sliced
1 tablespoon/15 ml paprika
pinch of cayenne pepper

2 tablespoons/30 ml wholemeal
    flour
$\frac{1}{2}$ pint/250 ml vegetable stock
1 vegetable stock cube
1 tablespoon/15 ml soy sauce
1 tablespoon/15 ml tomato purée
1 lb/450 g tomatoes, chopped
salt and pepper to taste
chopped parsley to garnish

Dumplings:
4 oz/125 g 100% wholemeal flour (self-raising)
$\frac{1}{4}$ teaspoon salt
1 oz/25 g butter or margarine
2 oz/50 g Cheddar cheese, grated
3 tablespoons/45 g parsley, chopped
2–3 fl oz/60–90 ml milk

Drain the beans, cover with fresh water and cook them until tender, about
35–40 minutes. Drain, reserving the liquid for stock. Heat the butter in a large
flameproof casserole. Add the onion and cook until transparent, then add the
garlic, leeks, carrot and mushrooms and cook gently for 4–5 minutes until the
vegetables have softened slightly. Stir in the paprika, cayenne and flour. Then
add the stock, stock cube, soy sauce, tomato purée, chopped tomatoes and salt
and pepper to taste. Bring to the boil, cover and simmer gently for 10 minutes.
Stir in the beans and bring mixture back to the boil. Then add the dumplings.
Cover with a tightly fitting lid and simmer gently for 20–25 minutes until the
dumplings are cooked. The casserole must simmer all the time once the
dumplings are added, but be careful not to have the heat too high, otherwise
it may catch on the bottom. Sprinkle generously with chopped parsley before
serving.

Dumplings:
Put the flour and salt in a basin. Rub in the butter until it resembles
breadcrumbs. Then stir in the grated cheese and parsley. Add just enough milk
to make a firm dough. Divide into 8 pieces and shape into dumplings.

POTATO PUDDING

Susan Barrie, hairdresser

Serves 4–6

6 large potatoes
2 eggs
1 large onion, grated
salt and pepper
2 tablespoons/30 ml self-raising flour

Grate potatoes into a colander, rinse and drain well. Mix all ingredients well and bind to a medium consistency. Grease a 10″ (25 cm) flat baking tin with oil, put the mixture in and flatten.

Bake for about 2 hours at 350F/180C/gas mark 4.

TABBOULEH

Anne-Sophie Wade, NSPCC Committee

Serves 4

8 oz/225 g cracked wheat (Burghul)
3 tablespoons/45 ml mint
6 spring onions
$\frac{1}{2}$ cucumber
2 large tomatoes
1 red sweet pepper
3 tablespoons/45 ml parsley, chopped

Dressing:
1 large clove garlic
juice of $\frac{1}{2}$ lemon
4 tablespoons/60 ml olive oil
salt and pepper

Boil some water and pour it over the cracked wheat and mint. Add water until the grain stops absorbing it.

In a salad bowl, put the crushed garlic, lemon juice, olive oil and salt and pepper, and mix well. Add the vegetables cut into cubes. Once the cracked wheat has become dry (it will double in size), add the dressing, and, lastly, the parsley.

FLAN DE POIVRONS

Patrick Milmo, QC

1 onion, finely cut
butter and oil
12 oz/350 g red peppers, cut and seeds removed
1 clove garlic, crushed
6 oz/175 g tomatoes, peeled and seeds removed
4 fl oz/100 ml fresh double cream
2 eggs, beaten
salt and pepper to taste

Gently fry the finely cut onion in a mixture of butter and oil. Add the peppers
and garlic, then the tomatoes. Cook in saucepan for about half an hour.
All liquid must have evaporated. Mix in liquidiser with fresh cream and eggs.
Pour the mixture into ramekins and cook in oven at 425F/220C/gas mark
7 for 20 minutes.

Serve cold.

Although it is called flan in French, there is no pastry involved.

It may be prepared in one larger mould and turned into a dish when cold to
serve.

If the preparation has not been entirely successful and the flan is not firm
enough, it is still delicious as a dip!

CORN PUDDING

Richard Wentworth, sculptor

'Imported from America, with gratitude to Beth Dow for her tuition.'

This dish goes very well with chicken, turkey or ham.

3 eggs
16 oz/475 ml single cream
16 oz/450 g fresh corn kernels, cut from cob; or drained, tinned corn.
1 tablespoon/15 ml butter, melted
2 teaspoons/10 g sugar
salt and freshly ground pepper
1 teaspoon/5 ml Worcester sauce

Heat oven to 350F/180C/gas mark 4.

Beat eggs and cream together until light, frothy and well blended.

Stir in corn, butter, sugar, salt, pepper and Worcester sauce.

Pour into buttered casserole and place in a large baking pan. Add 1″ (2.5 cm) of boiling water to the baking pan.

Bake for 1 hour, or until set.

Cool for 5 minutes before serving.

BREAD AND JAM FRITTERS	178	Mr Barber, caterer, HM Prison Pentonville
TOFFEE	178	Antonia Dugdale, ballet teacher
BEER DOUGH	179	Cinnamon Bakery
EVERTON'S TOFFEE	179	John Edwards, Douglas Pharmacy
DISGUSTING UPSIDE DOWN MATZA COFFEE CAKE	180	Michael Kuhn, Polygram
TOAST	180	Clive Anderson, TV personality
EVEREST BREAD	181	Charles Clarke, consultant neurologist
IRISH BREAD	182	T.A.J. Burnett, Keeper of Manuscripts the British Library
BANANA BREAD	182	Diana de Uphaugh, cook
MALTED BROWN LOAF	183	Giles Ridley, solicitor
BROWNIES	183	Jane Melrose, potter
GINGERBREAD	184	Chris Smith, MP, Islington South and Finsbury
BRAN FRUIT LOAF	184	Eric Holdstock, minister, Angel Baptist Church
BREAD SANDWICH	185	Posy Simmonds, The Guardian cartoonist
CHEESE SCONES	186	Cinnamon Bakery
LAMINGTONS	186	The Albion Pub, Finalist in the 1993 Evening Standard Pub of the Year
WHOLEMEAL SCONES	187	Victoria Plum Patisserie

BAKING & TEATIME

LUSCIOUS LEMON CURD CAKE	187	Ruth Thomson, children's writer
MY GRANDMOTHER'S VINEGAR CAKE	188	Jane Tuely, artist
FINNISH TOSCA CAKE	188	Cinnamon Bakery
POLISH POPPY-SEED CAKE	189	Barbara Bereza, Bereza's Beauty Salon
GINGER CAKE	190	Gill Wing, Le Café
MOIST CHOCOLATE CAKE	191	Sarah Knight, former cook to No. 10 Downing Street
SHORTBREAD	191	Dr Susan Wallington, art historian
ORANGE CAKE	192	Peter Bonsall, Parks and Recreation, Islington Council
VICARAGE FLAP-JACKS	192	Graham Claydon, Vicar, St Mary's Church, Islington
OATCAKES	193	Stephen Burroughs, Director of Education, Crafts Council
AUNTIE FREDA'S CHOCOLATE COCONUT BARS	193	Paula Pryke, florist
NANCY'S SCOTTISH TABLET	194	Eric Bush, retired swimming coach, Gallegos Club
MAYORESS SLICES	194	Susie Wilson, cook
TOFFEE CRISP	195	Allan's Shoe Shop
SANDWICHES	195	Sue Pollard, actress

BREAD AND JAM FRITTERS

Mr Barber, caterer, HM Prison Pentonville

4 slices bread
1 oz/25 g margarine
2 oz/50 g jam
caster sugar

Spread margarine and jam on bread to make jam sandwiches, cut in half.
Dip sandwich in batter and deep fry. Roll in caster sugar. Serve with custard.

Batter:
$\frac{1}{4}$ lb/125 g flour
pinch of salt
$\frac{1}{4}$ pint/150 ml water (tepid)
$\frac{1}{4}$ oz/5 g yeast
$\frac{1}{4}$ oz/5 g sugar

Sift flour and salt together, mix yeast and sugar together, add warm water.
Mix to smooth paste and allow to stand approximately 1 hour before using.

TOFFEE

Antonia Dugdale, ballet teacher

4 oz/125 g butter or margarine
8 oz/250 g golden syrup
1 tin sweetened condensed milk
8 oz/250 g granulated sugar

Melt the butter in thick-based saucepan and dissolve the sugar completely
before adding the syrup and condensed milk. Stir continuously over medium
heat until mixture changes to rich brown. To test toffee, drop a little into ice-
cold water (being careful not to let the toffee brown while you do this).
When the toffee sets hard in the water, it is ready.

Pour onto a lightly greased baking tray and score with a knife when slightly
cooled. Break up the toffee when cold and store in an airtight jar.

BEER DOUGH

Cinnamon Bakery

Makes 5 loaves – keep one, freeze the rest.

6 lbs/2.5 g flour	1½ pints/750 ml beer
1½ oz/40 g fat	1 pint/500 ml water
1½ oz/40 g salt	1 oz/25 g yeast

Mix flour, fat and salt together. Dissolve yeast in warm water. Then add water and beer to flour and knead to a stiff dough. Allow to stand covered with a cloth for 30 minutes. Knead again and shape into loaves. Allow to stand again until double their size. Wash with water and bake in hot oven, 450F/230C/ gas mark 8, for 30 minutes. Take out of oven and tap the bottoms. If they sound hollow they are baked, if not, return to oven for a bit longer.

EVERTON TOFFEE

John Edwards

John Edwards and his wife ran Douglas Pharmacy in Copenhagen Street for many years. People travelled long distances to purchase Dr Edwards' recipes for lotions and potions for many different ailments. He made up, among other things, wonderful cough mixtures, hand creams, face lotions, stomach powders and nappy rash creams. There was always something for everybody and it always worked.

Everton's toffee was a hand-made confection which was a strong favourite amongst young and old.

5 oz/125 g brown sugar	½ pint/250 ml water
1½ lb/750 g white sugar	5 oz/125 g butter
pinch of cream of tartar	1 teaspoon/5 ml oil of lemon

Boil the sugars, cream of tartar and water to 300F/150C. (Measure temperature using a sugar thermometer or until a little dropped on a cold plate solidifies immediately). Add butter, a little at a time, stirring gently, whilst still on the heat. Remove from heat and add the oil of lemon. Stir and pour into toffee tin. Score before it solidifies.

DISGUSTING UPSIDE DOWN MATZA COFFEE CAKE

Michael Kuhn, Polygram

1 box of Passover Matza
1 cup (not mug) of very sweet coffee
1 spoon
1 saucer

Discard half the cup of coffee.
Break Matza into $\frac{1}{4}''$ (6 mm) pieces.
Put quite a lot into the cup and soak.
Add sugar.
Ditto.

Press spoon down on soaked Matza and as spoon fills with coffee drink one spoon per layer.
Keep on making layers (remembering to add sugar to each layer) until cup is nearly full and coffee is either fully absorbed or drunk by chef.
Put saucer over cup and quickly invert. Tap bottom of cup.
A little cake of sodden, sweet, coffee-soaked Matza should now sit magnificently in the saucer.
Sprinkle with more sugar.
Eat noisily.
Spend next half hour digging bits of Matza from your wisdom teeth.

Warning: *only make in the morning at breakfast to get full effect of annoying rest of family.*

TOAST

Clive Anderson, TV personality

Cut 2 slices of bread from a loaf of your choice. (Quick method: take 2 slices from a sliced loaf). Put under grill or into toaster and toast for 2 or 3 minutes or until golden brown on both sides. Spread with butter or vegetable-oil-based substitute. Then spread with jam or (my favourite) marmalade.
Serve on a plate with a cup of tea.

Alternatively, I would recommend cooking leeks in this way.

EVEREST BREAD

Charles Clarke, consultant neurologist, St Bartholomew's Hospital

I am interested in medical aspects of high altitude mountaineering and have been on many expeditions to the Himalayas and to Everest. There is nothing like a hot loaf at 21,000 feet at the squalid Advance Base on the Tibetan side of Everest, but, God, it takes some time. First, get the Gaz roaring and a fug in the tent, prepare a simple oven over the stoves, for example a big dekski (a huge saucepan) full of pebbles, which will take two bread tins. *Take the day off climbing.*

2 lbs/900 g plain/brown flour
2 teaspoons/10 ml sugar
1 pint/400 ml milk (dried or fresh)
3 teaspoons/15 ml dried yeast

2 teaspoons/10 ml salt
4 oz/100 g butter or margarine
1 oz/20 g egg powder (or 2 fresh eggs)

Wash your filthy hands. Now wash them again.
Mix a dough with 4 oz/100 g flour, sugar, warm milk and yeast. Leave next to the stove (remember it's − 20°C outside) for half an hour. This gets the dough going. Have some tea and read a chapter of *Gorky Park*.

Tip in the rest of the ingredients and knead away for 10 minutes. The dough should be smooth and a bit sticky. Add a little water if necessary.

Stick it all in a black polybag, again near the stove for a further hour, or, in exceptional weather, in the warm windless sunshine, leave it outside. Snooze. The dough should have doubled in size. Slice it in half.

Place the dough in two tins (yes, grease them first, like you always do, otherwise it sticks). Leave for another half to one hour. Read more *Gorky Park*, cook supper, have more tea, open the whisky. Think about tomorrow and the load you'll have to carry, and the crevasses, and the avalanches, why you're here, and home. More whisky. Write home.

Then, bake for 40 minutes. Get the oven as hot as you can. The dekski bottom will be red hot. In Islington 425F/220C/gas mark 7.

When it's ready, let the tins cool a bit, *but make sure you stay around,* because if you don't, your friends will have eaten the bread in less time than it takes them to take off their crampons.

IRISH BREAD (Corisande Kemble)

T. A. J. Burnett, Keeper of Manuscripts, the British Library

This is one of the family recipes given to me by my mother. Corisande Kemble was her aunt.

$\frac{1}{2}$ lb/225 g plain flour
1 small teaspoon/5 ml salt
1 small teaspoon/5 ml bicarbonate of soda
2 teaspoons/10 ml vinegar
$\frac{1}{2}$ pint/250 ml milk

Mix flour, salt, and bicarbonate of soda together, getting all the lumps out. Add vinegar to milk and use to mix soft dough. Knead well. Bake in a greased tin for 40 minutes in a hot oven, 425F/220C/gas mark 7, then turn down.

BANANA BREAD

Diana de Uphaugh, cook

4 oz/125 g butter
7 oz/200 g caster sugar
2 eggs, size 2
3 medium bananas, mashed
1 teaspoon/5 ml lemon juice
2 oz/50 g walnuts, chopped
9 oz/250 g self-raising flour
3 level teaspoons/15 ml baking powder
pinch salt

Cream butter and sugar. Beat eggs well and add to butter.
Mix bananas with lemon and walnuts and add to mixture.
Sift flour, baking powder and salt into mixture.

Pour into greased loaf tin 4″ × 8″ × 2$\frac{3}{4}$″ (10 × 20 × 7 cms) and cook at 375F/190C/gas mark 5 for 1–1$\frac{1}{4}$ hours. Test with a skewer after 1 hour.

MALTED BROWN LOAF

Giles Ridley, solicitor

A very easy recipe which I have adapted – with a grateful acknowledgement for the original to Sam Wiggs.

Makes 3 loaves

Well oil 3 × 2 lb/900 g loaf tins. Using a fourth tin as a measure, three times fill it two thirds full with malted brown flour and empty into washing-up bowl in sink. Add 3 × 7 g sachets of dried yeast and 2 teaspoons/10 ml salt and mix. Add warm water from the tap and with a wooden spoon mix to a dough, not too dry and not too wet.

Split roughly amongst three prepared tins – fill roughly but press into corners with spoon. Sprinkle more flour liberally over tops. Put tins inside large dustbin bag in warm place – I use the warming drawer of an electric cooker – sitting them on a cooling rack. Leave for 1 hour or until mix has risen to top of the tin. Meanwhile pre-heat oven to 425F/220C/gas mark 7.

Bake for 35 minutes having reduced oven to 400F/200C/gas mark 6. Remove from tins and check loaves sound hollow underneath. If not 'pop back in oven' – as the cookbook writers say – for 5 minutes.

Very good for bread and pâté, cheese and prawns type Saturday lunch.

Freezes well. Toasts well a fortnight later!

BROWNIES   Jane Melrose, potter

4 oz/125 g cocoa	4 oz/125 g flour
4 oz/125 g butter or margarine	1 teaspoon/5 ml vanilla
4 eggs	4 oz/125 g walnuts, chopped
7 oz/200 g sugar	

Melt cocoa and butter and let cool. Beat eggs until thick. Gradually add sugar. Fold in butter and cocoa, then flour. Stir in vanilla and nuts.

Bake at 325F/170C/gas mark 3 for 40 minutes for a greased 9″ (23 cm) pan/20–25 minutes for a greased 13″ (33 cm) pan.

Cut into squares when cool and remove from pan.

GINGERBREAD   Chris Smith, MP Islington South and Finsbury

10 oz/300 g plain flour
1 flat teaspoon/5 ml bicarbonate of soda
1 flat teaspoon/5 ml ground ginger
1 flat teaspoon/5 ml cinnamon
6 oz/175 g demerara sugar

6 oz/175 g margarine or butter
6 oz/175 g black treacle
2 eggs and milk to mix
6 oz/175 g sultanas

Pre-heat oven to 325F/160C/gas mark 3.

Mix flour, bicarbonate, ginger, and cinnamon together. Cream the sugar and fat together, add treacle and cream further. Whisk eggs with milk, and add alternately with the dry ingredients to the creamed mixture. Add the sultanas.

Place in pre-heated oven for half an hour, then turn the oven down to 300F/150C/gas mark 2 and cook for a further hour. (For fan-assisted ovens reduce cooking time by 10 minutes).

BRAN FRUIT LOAF

Eric Holdstock, minister, Angel Baptist Church

This recipe is always a great favourite at church teas.

2 cups bran flakes
2 cups brown sugar
2 cups sultanas

2 cups milk
2 cups self-raising flour

Mix first four ingredients well and steep overnight.

Next day pre-heat oven 350F/180C/gas mark 4.

Lightly oil a 2 lb/900 g loaf tin and line base with greaseproof paper.

Add to mixture 2 cups self-raising flour and mix well.

Turn into prepared loaf tin and smooth top.

Bake for $1\frac{1}{4}$ hours until loaf is firm and hollow sounding when tapped. Leave to cool in tin. Turn out, slice and butter.

This loaf also freezes well.

KIT WRIGHT'S
BREAD SANDWICH

Take 3 slices of bread....

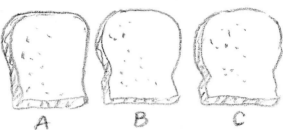

A   B   C

Butter A & B on one side
Butter C on both sides
Insert c between A & B

Posy Simmonds

CHEESE SCONES Cinnamon Bakery

8 oz/225 g self-raising flour
pinch of salt
1 level teaspoon/5 ml baking powder
1½ oz/40 g butter or margarine
3–4 oz/75–100 g mature Cheddar cheese, grated
1 level teaspoon/5 ml dry mustard
approx. ¼ pint/150 ml milk

Grease baking sheet. Sift flour, salt and baking powder and rub in fat until mixture resembles breadcrumbs. Stir in half the cheese and mustard, and enough milk to give a fairly soft light dough.

Roll out about 1¾" (2 cm) thick, cut into rounds with a 2" (5 cm) plain cutter.

Put onto baking sheet, brush the tops with milk and sprinkle with remaining cheese. Bake in oven at 425F/220C/gas mark 7 for about 10 minutes. When cold, cut in half and butter.

LAMINGTONS

The Albion Pub, Finalist in the 1993 Evening Standard Pub of the Year.

Make 3-minute sponge and cook in an oblong tin. Leave until next day, cut into squares and dip each in chocolate icing then roll in coconut. Leave to dry.

3-minute sponge:
Put into a basin one cup flour and ¾ cup sugar, break in 3 eggs,
add 3 tablespoons/45 ml melted butter and 2 tablespoons/30 ml milk.
Beat 3 minutes then stir in 2 teaspoons/10 ml baking powder.
Bake at 370F/190C/gas mark 5 for 15–20 minutes.

Chocolate icing:	6 tablespoons/90 ml boiling water
2 tablespoons/30 ml butter	12oz/350 g icing sugar
2 tablespoons/30 ml cocoa	few drops vanilla essence

Melt butter and cocoa in boiling water. Mix in sifted icing sugar, vanilla essence and beat well.

About 8 oz/225 g coconut is required for coating.

WHOLEMEAL SCONES

Victoria Plum, Patisserie

Makes 6–8 scones

4 oz/125 g strong flour
$\frac{1}{2}$ lb/225 g wholemeal flour
4 oz/125 g butter
$\frac{1}{2}$ oz/12 g baking powder
$\frac{1}{2}$ pint/250 ml milk
2 eggs

$\frac{1}{2}$ cup orange juice
2 pinches salt
3 oz/75 g walnuts
4 oz/125 g apricots, soaked and drained
4 oz/125 g sultanas

Put the flours and raising powder in a mixing bowl and rub in the butter.

Add the milk, eggs, orange juice and seasoning to make a softish dough. Do not overwork. Fold in all the fruits and nuts.

Scoop this soft mixture into small greased moulds or paper cases.

Bake in a pre-heated oven at 400F/200C/gas mark 7 for 20–25 minutes, depending on size of scones.

LUSCIOUS LEMON CURD CAKE Ruth Thomson, children's writer

This is a moist and tasty cake, which improves with keeping if your family and friends ever allow it to last beyond teatime!

6 oz/175 g butter or margarine
4 oz/125 g caster sugar
5 tablespoons/75 ml lemon curd

3 eggs
8 oz/225 g self-raising flour

Cream the butter and sugar together until you have a fluffy mixture. Stir in the lemon curd. Beat in the eggs, one by one. Lightly fold in the sifted flour.

Turn the mixture into a greased cake tin and bake in the centre of oven at 325F/160C/gas mark 3 for about an hour. (If you have a fan-assisted oven, check to see if a knife comes out cleanly after 50 minutes.)

Allow the cake to cool before turning it out.

To decorate, either sift some icing sugar on top or spread over some lemon water icing.

MY GRANDMOTHER'S VINEGAR CAKE

Jane Tuely, artist

This fruit cake never fails and has an unusual flavour – not at all vinegary!

12 oz/350 g flour
6 oz/175 g butter or margarine
6 oz/175 g soft brown sugar
8 oz/225 g mixed dried fruit
1 teaspoon/5 ml mixed spice
9 fl oz/250 ml milk
2 tablespoons/30 ml vinegar (wine or malt)
1 teaspoon/5 ml bicarbonate of soda

Preheat oven to 350F/180C/gas mark 4.

Rub the butter into the flour and add sugar, fruit and mixed spice.

Put vinegar into the milk and add the bicarbonate of soda (which causes it to froth up). Whisk with a fork, make a well in the centre of the dry ingredients and mix in very thoroughly. Grease an 8″(20 cm) cake tin, and put in cake mixture and level off the top – making a slight dent in the centre. Bake for $1\frac{1}{2}$ hours until the skewer comes out clean.

Improves if kept for a few days before eating.

FINNISH TOSCA CAKE

Cinnamon Bakery

5 oz/150 g butter	7 oz/200 g flour
5 oz/150 g sugar	$1\frac{1}{2}$ teaspoons/7.5 ml baking powder
2 eggs	2 fl oz/60 ml milk

Mix butter and sugar to fluffy mixture, then add one egg at a time. At the end add flour, baking powder and milk one after the other. Now pour into shallow greased baking tray and bake at 350F/180C/gas mark 4 for around 30 minutes.

Topping:
3 oz/75 g butter
3 oz/75 g almond flakes
2 oz/50 g sugar
3 tablespoons/45 g cream
1½ tablespoons/20 ml flour

Put all ingredients into a non-stick pan and boil mixture so that it is all well mixed together. Now pour mixture on top of the Tosca cake and return to oven for 15–20 minutes until the top is light brown.

POLISH POPPY SEED CAKE

Barbara Bereza, Bereza's Beauty Salon

This cake is delicious, impressive and easy to make. The crunchy, nutty texture of the poppy seeds blends wonderfully with the smoothness of the cake.

Poppy seeds are not always easy to find, but are always available from the Polish delicatessen in the basement of the local Polish church at 2 Devonia Road, London N1.

4 eggs
7 oz/200 g plain white flour
1½ teaspoons/7.5 ml baking powder
8 oz/225 g butter or margarine
8 oz/225 g granulated sugar
7 oz/200 g poppy seeds
almond essence

Separate the eggs. Mix the flour and baking powder. Using a spoon or beater, blend the butter and sugar well. Gradually add to this the flour mixture and egg yolks, one by one, until all the flour and egg yolks are mixed in. Mix well. Add the almond essence and poppy seeds. Mix well.

Beat egg whites until stiff and fold into mixture. Put into suitable baking tin (traditionally a 'Babka' tin – a fluted conical shape with a hole through the middle). However, a regular round tin will do.

Bake at 350F/180C/gas mark 4 for 40 minutes.

GINGER CAKE

Gill Wing, Le Café

8 oz/225 g butter
8 oz/225 g molasses or dark sugar
12 oz/350 g black treacle
2 tablespoons/30 ml whisky
8–10 oz/225–275 g plain flour (should be 8oz/225 g, but extra makes
    cake easier to cook!)
1 tablespoon/15 ml cinnamon
2 tablespoons/30 ml ground ginger
2 beaten eggs
1 teaspoon/5 ml bicarbonate of soda dissolved in warm milk
    (about 1–2 tablespoons/15–30 ml)

Optional extras:
handful of raisins
large tea or dessertspoon/10 ml chopped root ginger – excellent!
... or stem ginger – 2 or 3 pieces cut.

Pre-heat oven to 280F/145C/gas mark 1 or 2.

Cover an 8″ (20 cm) tallish tin with brown paper (not a flat cake tin).

Grease tin.

Cream butter and sugar together.

Add black treacle, whisky and optional extras.

Add sieved flour, mixed with spices, alternating with beaten egg. Mix lightly
with a metal spoon.

Lastly, add a teaspoon of bicarbonate of soda dissolved in milk, and mix
quickly into the cake. Put it in the lined and greased tin into the middle of
cool oven, for 2–3 hours. Best if removed whilst softish. DO NOT HURRY.

Cool slowly in tin first then extract.

Do not be alarmed if it is moist and spills over and collapses – this is normal!

MOIST CHOCOLATE CAKE

Sarah Knight, former cook to No. 10 Downing Street

6 oz/175 g plain flour
2 oz/50 g cocoa
4 oz/125 g soft brown sugar
4 oz/125 g golden syrup

4 oz/125 g margarine
5 fl oz/125 ml milk
1 egg, beaten into milk
1½ teaspoons/7.5 ml bicarbonate of soda

Filling:
2 oz/50 g butter or margarine
1 dessertspoon/10 ml cocoa

3 oz/75 g icing sugar, sifted
vanilla essence

Pre-heat oven to 375F/190C/gas mark 5.

Sift flour and cocoa into a bowl. Melt sugar, syrup and margarine together. Remove from heat, add milk, egg mixture and bicarbonate of soda. Stir until combined. Add mixture to flour and stir until smooth. Spread mixture into either a pair of greased, lined sandwich tins or one deeper tin.

Bake for 20–30 minutes or until springy. Sides of cake should leave the tin.

Filling: beat all ingredients together until light and creamy. Sandwich cakes together with filling and spread over the top.

SHORTBREAD

Dr Susan Wallington, art historian

4 oz/125 g butter or margarine
2 oz/50 g sugar
4 oz/125 g plain flour
2 oz/50 g ground rice

Cream the butter and sugar. Sieve in the flour and ground rice. Put the mixture into a round, greased tin. Decorate the top with almonds, if you wish. Bake in the middle of a medium oven, 380F/190C/gas mark 5, for about half an hour.

The ground rice gives this recipe the characteristic texture.

It originated from Syllabub's column – I think it was in the News Chronicle.

ORANGE CAKE

Peter Bonsall, Parks and Recreation, Islington Council

8 oz/225 g margarine	Topping:
8 oz/225 g caster sugar	1 lemon
4 eggs	1 orange
8 oz/225 g self-raising flour	3 oz/75 g caster sugar
juice of $\frac{1}{2}$ lemon	2 teaspoons/10 ml vanilla essence

Cream the margarine and sugar until fluffy. Add the eggs, one by one, adding a little of the flour as you go to prevent curdling. Add the rest of the flour. Add the juice of half a lemon (it will look like it has curdled, but don't worry). Thoroughly grease a round (or square) tin and line the bottom of the tin with silicon paper. Add mixture and cook at 325F/170C/gas mark 3 for $1\frac{1}{4}$ hours.

Leave in tin to cool for at least $\frac{3}{4}$ hour and then turn out onto wire tray.

Meanwhile grate zest of both the orange and lemon into a bowl, then add the juices of both. Add the caster sugar and vanilla essence. Before cake is completely cool, make a few holes in the top with a skewer and pour the mixture on to the top of the cake.

VICARAGE FLAP-JACK

Graham Claydon, vicar, St Mary's Church, Islington

4 oz/125 g butter or margarine
4 oz/125 g soft brown sugar
1 generous tablespoon/15 ml golden syrup
4 oz/125 g self-raising flour
4 oz/125 g porridge oats

To mix – Vicarage method. Melt the butter, sugar and syrup in a large pan and stir in the flour and oats. Press into a flat baking tray and cook at 350F/180C/gas mark 4 for anything between 10–20 minutes, depending on mood, telephone, visitors, etc.

OATCAKES

Stephen Burroughs, Director of Education, Crafts Council

A go anywhere, eat any time, survival snack.

$\frac{1}{2}$ oatflakes and $\frac{1}{2}$ butter or margarine by weight
Add sugar to taste

Mix as for pastry and press into a baking tin. Bake at 425F/220C/gas mark 7
until golden brown.

Variations: add chopped cherries, nuts, coconut, chocolate chips, etc.

AUNTIE FREDA'S CHOCOLATE COCONUT BARS

Paula Pryke, florist

4 oz/125 g margarine
2 oz/50 g sugar
1 teacup flour
2 teaspoons/10 ml cocoa
1 teacup desiccated coconut
chocolate for icing

Cream margarine and sugar, add flour, cocoa and coconut. Spread mixture
into a baking tin.

Bake until firm.

Ice with melted chocolate and cut into fingers. Leave to cool before removing.

NANCY'S SCOTTISH TABLET

Eric Bush, retired swimming coach, Gallegos Club

1 teacup milk (not skimmed)
2 oz/50 g butter
2 lbs/900 g granulated sugar
small tin condensed milk
1 tablespoon/15 ml syrup
few drops vanilla essence

Put milk, butter and sugar in strong pan, heat and when dissolved add condensed milk. Bring slowly to the boil stirring all the time. Add syrup and boil gently for 5 minutes. Test the mixture in cold water, take pot off heat, add vanilla essence and beat for 4–5 minutes.

Pour mixture into a tray and allow to cool.

MAYORESS SLICES

Susie Wilson, cook

1 cup flour
1 cup porridge oats
$\frac{3}{4}$ cup brown sugar
$\frac{1}{4}$ cup coconut flakes (or 1 oz/25 g slice of coconut ice)
1 heaped tablespoon/15 ml chocolate powder
5 oz/150 g margarine
melted cooking chocolate to decorate
hundreds and thousands

Mix all the dry ingredients together. Melt margarine and add to the mixture. Pour into a small Swiss roll baking tin and bake in a hot oven, 350F/180C/ gas mark 4, for 20 minutes. When cool, spread evenly with melted chocolate and hundreds and thousands. When chocolate sets, slice up into small squares.

TOFFEE CRISP

Allan Shoe Shop

Allans have been fitting shoes to the residents of Islington since 1869.

4 oz/125 g marshmallows
4 oz/125 g margarine
4 oz/125 g plain toffee (a slab of wrapped toffees)
Rice Crispies

Melt the first three ingredients in a large bowl over a saucepan of boiling water, until they blend into a thick, smooth, creamy sauce.

Remove from the heat and add as many Rice Crispies as will fold in.

Press into a greased tin approx 10″ (25 cm) square. Leave to cool, then cut into squares.

Popular with adults as well as children.

I have made this using the microwave – much quicker. Melt the toffee a little first, add margarine and marsh mallows. Remove and beat into thick creamy sauce , then add Rice Crispies.

SANDWICHES

Sue Pollard, actress

'Unfortunately, I'm a terrible cook. I don't do anything well really. I only make sandwiches and so here is a suggestion. Take two slices of bread, spread them with butter, Flora or a low fat margarine, and add a filling of your choice, and enjoy it when you eat it!'

SUPPER PARTY	198	Gill Coleridge, literary agent
PARTY PUDDINGS	199	Gill Coleridge, literary agent
SUMMER PATE	200	Susan Palmer, NSPCC Committee
AUBERGINE CAVIAR	201	Clare McCann, NSPCC Committee
SMOKED SALMON PATE	201	Olga Conway, The Upper Street Fish Shop
SALADE COMPOSEE AU SAUMON FUMEE	202	Marina Milmo, solicitor
PIG'S BLOOD PANCAKES	202	Paula Rego, artist
TARAMASALATA	204	Emily Lloyd, actress
MICHAEL'S MUSHROOMS	205	Robin Richmond, artist
CHEESE PASTRIES	205	Joan Dunnett, artist
CHEESE BISCUITS	206	Miles and Sheila Thompson, The Islington Society
STILTON SLICE	206	Mary Gibson, headteacher, Yerbury School, Tufnell Park

GIVING A PARTY

TARTE A LA BIERE	207	Sophie Grigson, cookery writer
STRAWBERRY TART	208	Jacqueline Latham, NSPCC Committee
SLICE OF HEAVEN	209	Annie Dugan-Webster, Dugan's Chocolate Shop
CHOCOLATE PATE	210	Annie Dugan-Webster, Dugan's Chocolate Shop
TIRA-ME-SU (PICK ME UP)	211	Mark Elder, conductor
THE ULTIMATE HOT CHOCOLATE	211	Annie Dugan-Webster, Dugan's Chocolate Shop
DAMS GIN	212	Eric Bush, retired swimming coach, Gallegos Club
SLOE GIN	212	Brian Palmer, BP Chemicals
"FRENCH 75"	213	Derek Birdsall, Omnific
WHITE WINE FRUIT CUP	214	Alan Warner, financial advisor
MULLED WINE	214	Richard Wallington, barrister
APPLE WINE	215	Brian Palmer, BP Chemicals

SUPPER PARTY for 20 plus . . .

Gill Coleridge, literary agent

For those of us who live in tall, thin houses without enormous rooms, who nonetheless love to have lots of friends to supper, the only answer is an extremely simple meal, easily eaten with only fork and plate, which can be carried and eaten whilst sitting or standing. It is also important to have an easily served meal, so minimum time is spent in the kitchen.

Here is a suggestion for a winter supper party, with quantities for about 20.

Starters: With drinks I usually serve stuffed vol-au-vent, small ones (I buy the frozen ones). Stuff with mushrooms, chopped finely into a white bechamel sauce; and some prawns also in a bechamel sauce to which you've added some paprika. The sauce can be made before and frozen. On the day, cook the pastry cases, stuff with the fillings and heat through in a low oven.

Main Course: I usually serve two casseroles so there is a choice. Here is one of my favourites; (it doesn't seem to have a name, I've developed it over the years from a recipe of my mother's). It can be cooked the day before and re-heated on the day.

PORK CASSEROLE

Serves 20

4 oz/125 g butter or margarine
5–6 lbs/2.25–2.75 kg lean pork, chopped and diced
   (it depends how hungry your friends are!)
5 medium onions, chopped finely
3 dessertspoons/30 ml paprika
3 dessertspoons/30 ml flour
6 teaspoons/30 ml tomato purée
3 glasses sherry
1½ pints/750 ml good jellied stock (Campbells beef consommé is excellent –
   use 3 tins)
salt and pepper
1½ lb/675 g button mushrooms, sliced
3 dessertspoons/30 ml cornflour
20 fl oz/600 ml cream, double or single

Soften the onions in butter, then add meat and fry gently till coloured. Stir in paprika and flour (take care it doesn't stick; if need be, add a knob more butter). Stir in tomato purée and sherry, make sure the sauce is smooth, then add the stock. Season with salt and black pepper. Stir slowly over heat, making sure the ingredients are properly blended, and bring gently to the boil. Put into thick casserole with lid, adding the sliced mushrooms. Cook in oven for about 2 hours; first 20 minutes at 400F/200C/gas mark 6; then, having checked it is gently bubbling, turn down to simmer gently 250F/120C/gas mark $\frac{1}{2}$.

Just before serving, take out of oven. Once the bubbles have stopped, stir in the cornflour and the cream. Serve with hot tagliatelle, and, if you want a vegetable, red cabbage is delicious. That too, could be cooked the day before. I do it chopped up in a Le Creuset casserole, with onions, apple and vinegar (Katie Stewart has an excellent recipe in both her Cookbook and Times Cookbook).

PARTY PUDDINGS

Gill Coleridge, literary agent

I'm inclined to keep these simple, but with a choice of at least two or three. Sometimes I do meringues or profiteroles, and often a fruit salad. But invariably I do at least a couple of soufflés, which aren't technically soufflés I'm told – probably they should be called mousses – but it's a recipe much-honed by my mother and unfailingly successful.

LEMON SOUFFLE

Serves 8–10

9 eggs
1 sachet Davis gelatine (sometimes I put in a bit more, just to be on
   the safe side)
12 oz/350 g caster sugar
5 large lemons

Separate the eggs. Put the gelatine to soak in a cup, with a teaspoonful of water. Add the sugar to the yolks and beat hard (I use a Kenwood mixer) until white and creamy. Grate some of the skin of the lemons (finely) and add, then squeeze the juice of the lemons, add to mixture and beat again. Put the cup containing gelatine into small saucepan with water, stir gently (it may be necessary to add another drop or two of water) and when it is dissolved and clear, pour quickly into mixture, then beat again. Leave in a cool place, and, when it is just beginning to set (ie., getting firm round the edges), then beat the whites until firm, and fold gently into the mixture with a metal spoon. Pour into a large serving bowl and decorate with blobs of whipped cream.

APRICOT SOUFFLE

Same as above, but using dried apricots, and a little less sugar or it is too sweet. For these quantities soak 1 lb/450 g apricots, cook in a pressure cooker, then liquidise. You need to have about $\frac{1}{2}$ pint/250 ml apricot purée.

BLACKCURRANT SOUFFLE

Again, you need to cook the fruit, using about 2 lbs/900 g blackcurrants to make about $\frac{1}{2}$ pint/250 g or more of strong purée.

CHOCOLATE SOUFFLE

Bring $\frac{1}{2}$ pint/250 g milk gently to boil with 6 dessertspoons/60 ml of cocoa, stirring gently so it is completely smooth. When off the boil, pour into beaten egg/sugar mixture (pour through a sieve just in case any lumps are left). Use less sugar than in the lemon and blackcurrant version – I use 1 oz/25 g per egg.

SUMMER PATE

Susan Palmer, NSPCC Committee

Serves 8–10

6 oz/175 g butter
8 oz/225 g fresh soft herring roe
salt and fresh pepper

juice of small lemon
4 teaspoons parsley, finely chopped

Melt roughly half the butter in frying pan, add roe and season. Fry gently for 5 minutes, turning the roe over occasionally. Remove pan from heat and put roes and butter into mixing bowl. Beat until smooth. Beat in remaining softened butter, lemon juice and parsley. Chill.

To mix in a blender, add the ingredients separately; and stir in parsley.

AUBERGINE CAVIAR

Clare McCann, NSPCC Committee

A dip which is always a hit at parties. It is quick and easy to make and utterly delicious. The recipe is from *Abby Mandel's 'Cuisinart Classroom'*; she is an American cook well-known for her skill with the food processor.

Makes 2 cups

1 large aubergine (1 lb/450 g unpeeled, trimmed)

1 cup parsley	$\frac{1}{2}$ teaspoon/2.5 ml dried oregano
1 large clove garlic	$\frac{1}{2}$ teaspoon/2.5 ml dried dill weed
1 small piece of onion ($\frac{1}{2}$ oz/15g)	2 teaspoons/10 ml lemon juice
$\frac{1}{2}$ cup mayonnaise	1 teaspoon/5 ml salt
$\frac{1}{2}$ teaspoon/2.5 ml dried basil	freshly ground pepper

Pre-heat oven to 350F/180C/gas mark 4.

Bake aubergine for 50 minutes, or until soft. Let it cool and cut into quarters. Using the metal blade on your food processor first mince the parsley, second add garlic and onion, third add the aubergine and purée the mixture. Finally add the remaining ingredients and process the machine for 5 seconds. Check the seasoning.

Put into a bowl and chill. Serve with crudité, tortilla chips and/or cheese biscuits.

SMOKED SALMON PATE

Olga Conway, The Upper Street Fish Shop

8 oz/225 g smoked salmon
4 tablespoons/60 ml double cream
black pepper, freshly ground
juice of 1 lemon

Mix the smoked salmon, double cream and lemon juice to taste in a blender for long enough to make a smooth paste. Add black pepper to taste, and a little salt, if necessary. Pipe onto small plates and garnish or use as a dip. Serve with crackers.

SALADE COMPOSEE AU SAUMON FUMEE

Marina Milmo, solicitor

Serves 8

1 round lettuce	Dressing:
1 cucumber	French mustard
2 avocado pears (or 1 large one)	wine vinegar
16 quails eggs	olive oil (or a mixture of olive and
3 tomatoes	vegetable oil)
8 oz/225 g smoked salmon	fresh dill
	salt and pepper

Wash the lettuce, drain and shred. Peel cucumber and cut in small thin strips. Peel avocado pears, remove stones and slice, widthways. Hard boil quails eggs and peel. Cut tomatoes in 8 pieces. Cut smoked salmon into strips. Spread shredded lettuce on each plate, add cut cucumber, cover with sliced avocados. Add strips of smoked salmon, curled on each plate, with 2 quails eggs and 3 tomato pieces.

If prepared in advance, cover each plate with cling film and refrigerate. Remove from refrigerator a little while before serving and cover with salad dressing at the last moment.

PIG'S BLOOD PANCAKES

Paula Rego, artist

a bowl full of pig's blood
self-raising flour
aniseed
pine nuts

Mix the blood with the flour a little at a time until it becomes a thick paste. Put in the sweet herbs and nuts. Cover and let it rest for at least an hour. Deep fry in olive oil a spoonful at a time. Eat them with red wine.

If you don't have pig's blood you can use chicken's, but it is not as nice.

Paula Rego

TARAMASALATA

Emily Lloyd, actress

I have chosen the recipe of Taramasalata as, apart from enjoying this appetiser, it's the only dish my mother has ever managed to achieve. My after-school snack during childhood was invariably Taramasalata!

When I return to live in my home town of Islington, which I love, I hope to have more time to discover the art of cooking and avoid the pre-packed supermarket cuisine.

Serves 4–6

1 small jar smoked cod's roe
6 slices white bread
$\frac{1}{4}$ Spanish onion, grated
1–2 cloves garlic, mashed
8 tablespoons/120 ml olive oil
juice of 1 lemon
1 tablespoon/15 ml parsley, finely chopped
green olives
hot toast

Place cod's roe in a mortar. Trim crusts from bread; soak bread in water; squeeze and add to cod's roe. Pound mixture to a smooth paste. Stir in grated onion and garlic. Then add olive oil and lemon juice alternately in small amounts, stirring well, until mixture acquires a smooth, uniform consistency. Strain through a fine sieve. (The above can be done in an electric blender, in which case the mixture does not need to be sieved).

Serve in a salad bowl; sprinkle with finely-chopped parsley and garnish with green olives. Serve with hot toast. 2″ (5 cm) lengths of crisp celery stuffed with this mixture served as a light appetiser are very good.

MICHAEL'S MUSHROOMS

Robin Richmond, artist

1 punnet oyster mushrooms, or ceps if you can get them.
2 fl oz/60 ml lemon juice
5 oz/150 g plain white flour, seasoned with salt and pepper
1 egg
2 fl oz/60 ml milk
6 oz/175 g fine breadcrumbs
sunflower oil for frying

Dip:
Lite crème fraiche or fromage frais
salt and pepper to taste
Sainsbury's Condiverde

Dip mushrooms in lemon juice. Coat in seasoned flour. Coat in beaten egg and milk. Coat in breadcrumbs. Shallow fry in sunflower oil. Drain on kitchen towel. Sprinkle with lemon juice and salt. Can be kept warm in low oven. Lovely with dip.

CHEESE PASTRIES

Joan Dunnett, artist

2 oz/50 g flour
2 oz/50 g butter, cut in pieces
2 oz/50 g strong Cheddar or Parmesan cheese
salt and paprika
1 egg

Put flour, butter, cheese, salt and paprika into a bowl and mix with spoon until dough is smooth and firm (or in a mixer). Leave for 1 hour. Roll out thinly. Cut into rounds. Glaze with egg. Bake in a moderately hot oven, 375F/ 190C/gas mark 5, for 10 minutes.

CHEESE BISCUITS

Miles and Sheila Thompson, The Islington Society

Makes 40

4 oz/125 g soft margarine
3½ oz/90 g self-raising flour
2 oz/50 g semolina
½ teaspoon/2.5 g salt
½ teaspoon/2.5 g dry mustard
4 oz/125 g strong Cheddar cheese, grated
4 oz/125 g cashew nuts, for decoration

Mix everything together, except the nuts, in a food processor. Put 40 small blobs on a baking sheet. Stick half a cashew on each blob. Bake at 350F/180C/gas mark 4 for 15–20 minutes.

Excellent for nibbling with drinks.

STILTON SLICE

Mary Gibson, headteacher, Yerbury School, Tufnell Park

1 lb/450 g packet puff pastry
½ lb/225 g Stilton cheese, or Cheddar cheese for children
1 egg
pepper, poppy or sesame seeds (optional)

Roll out the pastry to a large square. Beat the egg into the crumbled Stilton cheese. Season with black pepper. Put the mixture onto the pastry and brush edges of pastry with milk. Fold the pastry over like a parcel. Brush top with milk and sprinkle over the poppy or sesame seeds. Bake in a moderate oven, 350F/180C/gas mark 4, for 30 minutes.

This is delicious cut into fingers and served with drinks, or into larger portions and served with a salad.

TARTE A LA BIERE

Sophie Grigson, cookery writer

Serves 10–12

Pastry:
1 lb/450 g flour
$\frac{1}{4}$ teaspoon/1.5 ml salt
4 oz/100 g caster sugar
$5\frac{1}{2}$ oz/150 g ground almonds
11 oz/300 g butter
4 eggs
$\frac{1}{2}$ teaspoon/2.5 ml vanilla essence

Filling:
$5\frac{1}{2}$ oz/150 g granulated sugar
3 eggs
$\frac{1}{4}$ pint/150 ml Bière de Garde (I use Sainsbury's Bière de Garde, but another lager could be used instead)
1 oz/30 g butter, melted and cooled to tepid

To make the pastry: sift the flour with the salt. Mix with caster sugar and almonds. Rub in butter. Add eggs and vanilla essence and mix to a soft dough. Knead briefly, then wrap in clingfilm and chill for $\frac{1}{2}$ hour. Bring back to room temperature and roll out to a thickness of about $\frac{1}{2}''$ (1 cm). Line a 11–12″ (28–30 cm) tart tin with the pastry. Prick the base all over with a fork and sprinkle with the $5\frac{1}{2}$ oz/150 g granulated sugar. Cover loosely with foil and bake for 15 minutes at 350F/180C/gas mark 4. Remove foil and bake for a further 15 minutes.

When the pastry is almost done, make the filling. Beat the eggs lightly, then gradually beat in the beer and melted butter. Pour over the sugar in the baked pastry case and return to the oven for 15–20 minutes until just set. Leave to cool completely.

STRAWBERRY TART

Jacqueline Latham, NSPCC Committee

This is an easy recipe that takes only 50 minutes to prepare.

Serves 8

1 ½ lb/700 g strawberries	4 tablespoons/60 ml kirsch or Grand Marnier
4 oz/125 g sugar	

Shortcrust pastry:
1 egg
2 oz/50 g sugar
1 pinch salt
8 oz/225 g flour
4 oz/125 g butter

Cream:
2 eggs
3 oz/75 g sugar
2 oz/50 g flour
½ pint/250 ml milk
1 oz/25 g butter
1 or 2 tablespoons/15 or 30 ml kirsch
   or Grand Marnier

Wash the strawberries, drain and remove stalks. Put in a bowl with sugar and kirsch or Grand Marnier.

Heat the oven to 350F/180C/gas mark 4.

For the pastry, mix beaten egg with the sugar and pinch of salt. Add the flour in one go, mix well – the appearance of the mixture will be granular. Put on a board and incorporate the butter, working together with the fingers of one hand until a ball is formed. Leave to rest for a moment.

Roll out the pastry on a floured board, line an 11″ (28 cm) greased tin with the pastry and prick the bottom with a fork. Cook in the preheated oven for 15–20 minutes. Cool in the tin, then unmould on a flat dish.

For the cream, mix the eggs with the sugar and flour and stir in the hot milk. Put on gentle heat until boiling point, stirring all the time.

Remove from the heat, add butter and kirsch or Grand Marnier. Pour the cream into a jug and leave to cool, stirring from time to time. Spread cream over the base of the pastry case and garnish with the strawberries.

You can spread warmed gooseberry jelly on the strawberries to give a professional finish. Raspberries, gooseberries, grapes or redcurrants can be used instead of strawberries and should be left uncooked. You can also use a ready-made base.

SLICE OF HEAVEN

Annie Dugan-Webster, Dugan's Chocolates

Makes 30 pieces

Base:
8 oz/250 g unsalted butter
5 oz/150 g dark chocolate, melted
4 × 2 oz/60 g eggs
1 lb/500 g caster sugar
5 oz/150 g plain flour

Topping:
8 oz/250 g unsalted butter
14 oz/400 g icing sugar
4 oz/100 g dark chocolate, melted
4 oz/100 g marshmallows, chopped
4 oz/100 g dark chocolate, chopped into small pieces
4 oz/100 g Macadamia nuts

Pre-heat oven to 325F/160C/gas mark 3.

Grease a Swiss roll tray and line with baking paper.

To make base – mix the melted butter with the chocolate and whisk eggs until smooth. Add the sugar and flour and stir until smooth. Spread the mixture into the prepared tin and bake for 45 minutes.

To make topping – while the base is baking, mix the butter and icing sugar together until light and fluffy. Add the melted chocolate to the butter mix and then fold through the chopped marshmallows, chocolate and nuts. Once baked, allow the slice to cool slightly, but while still warm spread the topping evenly over the base. Refrigerate for 24 hours.

Slice into portions using a hot knife.

CHOCOLATE PATE

Annie Dugan-Webster, Dugan's Chocolate Shop

Serves 20

4 oz/125 g shortbread biscuits
6 oz/175 g dark chocolate
2½ fl oz/75 ml water
2 oz/50 g caster sugar
1 tablespoon/15 ml cocoa
6 oz/175 g unsalted butter
2 oz/50 g brazil nuts, chopped
2 oz/50 g pistachio nuts, chopped
2 oz/50 g glacé pineapple
2 oz/50 g glacé apricots
2½ tablespoons/135 ml Grand Marnier
zest of 1 orange
zest of 1 lemon
1 egg
2 egg yolks

Crush the biscuits finely and melt the chocolate. Put the water and sugar in a saucepan and bring slowly to the boil and boil for 5 minutes. Allow to cool slightly.

Cream the cocoa and butter together until light and fluffy. Mix in the chopped nuts, fruits and crushed biscuits.

Add the chocolate to the boiled syrup and stir until smooth, then add the Grand Marnier, lemon and orange zests and finally the egg and egg yolks. Fold in the butter and cocoa mixture and stir until well combined.

Line a 9″ (23 cm) springform cake tin with cling film and pour in mixture and press firmly into tin and smooth the top. Refrigerate for 24 hours before unmoulding and serving in very fine slices with coffee.

TIRA-ME-SU (Pick Me Up)

Mark Elder, conductor

4 egg yolks
4 dessertspoons/40 g sugar
9 oz/250 g Marscapone cheese
strong coffee
4 beaten egg whites
brandy or rum
sponge biscuits
chocolate to sprinkle

Mix egg yolks and sugar together, add Marscapone and mix. Add 3 tablespoons/45 ml of cold coffee and mix. Add beaten egg whites. Soak biscuits in brandy and line a bowl or bread-baking size dish, ie. either do layers and alternate, or line with biscuits and pour mixture on top.

Sprinkle whole thing with chocolate powder, or grated, and leave in the fridge.

THE ULTIMATE HOT CHOCOLATE

Annie Dugan-Webster, Dugan's Chocolate Shop

Makes 2 cups

2 oz/50 g dark chocolate
2 teaspoons/10 ml cocoa
2 teaspoons/10 ml drinking chocolate
2 teaspoons/10 ml Grand Marnier
12 fl oz/360 ml milk
6 marshmallows
cinnamon for dusting

Melt chocolate, add cocoa, drinking chocolate and Grand Marnier. Pour boiled milk over chocolate mixture and whisk until light and frothy. Pour into mugs – add 3 marshmallows to each and dust with cinnamon.

For even better results, leave to rest overnight before adding marshmallows. The mixture will then be soft and velvety. But, some of us can't wait that long.

DAMS GIN

Eric Bush, retired swimming coach, Gallegos Club

There are thousands of damsons available in parks, rough ground and friends' or neighbours gardens. Sometimes a ladder, or at least a walking stick can guarantee a good supply. Collect at the beginning of September when the fruit is plump but not over-ripe.

Remove stalks and thoroughly wash the fruit.

Place in a saucepan, cover with water and gently boil; this causes all the stones to come to the top, when it is easy to pick them out with a wooden spatula.

Prepare jars (used gin bottles are best). When the fruit is cool, place in the jars and top up with gin.

Label with date and keep for 2 years.

The result is a beautifully sharp, fruity alcoholic drink fit for all.

SLOE GIN

Brian Palmer, BP Chemicals

One Christmas my parents' neighbours offered us this delicious and powerful drink in sherry glasses. Though they lived but a few hundred yards away and it was long before the breathaliser, we had to leave the car for collection later and walk home. This Victorian recipe is memorable for its simplicity and quantities – take a gallon of sloes and a gallon of gin! Prick, cut or bruise the sloes, soak in the gin for three months. Pass through a coffee filter and bottle. Makes 5 bottles.

Our neighbours fed the sloes to the chickens; they claimed that within minutes the poor birds were headless and legless, and did not lay again for a month!

"FRENCH 75"

Derek Birdsall, Omnific

Named after the most destructive field gun used in the 1914–18 War,
this is an economical, delicious, and destructive summer cocktail.

Almost fill a wineglass with cold, cheap, sparkling white wine
(French or Italian).
Add 2 teaspoonsful of gin and a teaspoonful of fresh lemon juice.

Stir.
Drink.

Dissolve.

WHITE WINE FRUIT CUP

Alan Warner, financial advisor

Serves 10

fresh fruit (cherries, peaches, raspberries or strawberries)
6 oz/150 g caster sugar
4 tablespoons/60 ml brandy
2 bottles Sauvignon
soda water according to desired strength

Slice fruit and put into a bowl. Add sugar and brandy. Pour in chilled white wine. Add soda water.

Very popular with our Islington friends.

MULLED WINE

Richard Wallington, barrister

1 orange
cloves
3 bottles red wine
cup of China tea (keemun or Lapsang, not Earl Grey)
$\frac{1}{2}$ bottle sweet sherry
$\frac{1}{2}$ bottle brown rum
brown sugar
powdered cinnamon

Bake the orange stuck with cloves in a slow oven for about an hour. Cut the orange into four. Add to the wine and simmer for about 20 minutes. Add a cup of strong China tea, then add the sherry and rum, and brown sugar and cinnamon to taste, keeping the drink warm.

APPLE WINE

Brian Palmer, BP Chemicals

Makes $4\frac{1}{2}$–5 gallons

15 lbs/6 kg apples, approximately
2 × 5 gallon buckets
12 lbs/4.75 kg granulated sugar
a good pinch of yeast (Type 67)
3 teaspoons/15 ml yeast nutrient

Half fill a 5-gallon plastic bucket with roughly chopped apples and fill with water. Cover. Turn in the top layer daily as it goes brown and leave to soak until apples are soft; one to three weeks depending on the lateness of the season. Remove the apple pieces with a sieve and drain the liquid through a coarse muslin. Add $2\frac{1}{2}$ lbs/1.1 kg sugar to each gallon of liquid for a dry wine, $3\frac{1}{2}$ lbs/1.6 kg for a sweet wine. At the same time add the yeast and nutrient preferably having 'started' it in a sugar solution the day before. Replace the lid of the bucket, stir daily, and after about five days when the fermentation has somewhat subsided, transfer to gallon jars or barrels sealed with fermentation locks. The larger containers have always proved more successful.

For the technically inclined, the progress of fermentation can be followed with a hygrometer, otherwise leave in the garden shed and the wine will be ready for bottling by March. Use a siphon to remove the clear liquid from the leys, then cork up in gallon jars or barrels. The best result is obtained by bottling the wine just before fermentation has finished at a specific gravity of 1003 or so. The fermentation will recommence with the warmer weather and if the corks don't blow the result almost beats champagne. Apple wine can be drunk by mid-summer but is best the following year. It keeps for many years, if ever it gets the chance.

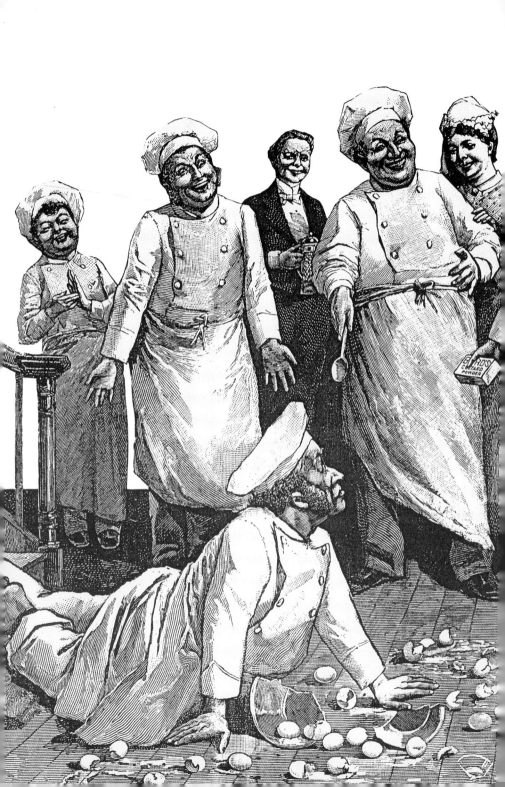

INDEX

Abbot Ale batter. Cod in..... 68

All-Purpose Italian Sauce 43

Anchovy:-
  Cold Scotch Woodcock 15

Apple:-
  Apple and Mincemeat Steam
  Pudding 151
  Apple Cheesecake 137
  Apple Wine 215
  Dutch Apple Pie 144
  Katrina's Apple Cake 140
  Serendipitous Parsnip and Apple 167
  Tarte Tatin 153

Apricot:-
  An Abundance of Apricots 146
  Apricot Souffle 200

Artichoke:-
  Ferrari's Pasta al Carcioli 53

Asparagus:-
  Supremes of Chicken with
  Asparagus 78

Athole Brose. MacGregor's 139

Aubergine:-
  Aubergine Caviar 201
  Aubergine Pie 161
  Aubergines and Tomatoes 38
  Pasta in Aubergine Sauce 52

Auntie Freda's Chocolate Coconut
  Bars 193

Avocado Creams 16

Bacon:-
  Bigos (Polish Hunter's Stew) 123
  Goat's Cheese and Bacon Salad 31
  Poor Man's Supper 120
  Salad of hot potatoes, bacon, onions
  with escarole 119
  Scrambled eggs and bacon 126
  Vegetable and Bacon Stew 129

Baked Beans. Homemade 34

Baked Fudge Pudding 143

Baked Lemon Chicken 86

BAKING AND TEATIME 176–195
Banana:-
    Banana Bread 182
    Banana Flambé 155
    Banana Fool 140
    Banana Soya Dessert 142
    Mackerel and Banana Curry 62
Bang Bang Chicken 84
Basil:-
    Pesto alla Genovese 44
Beans:-
    West Indian Rice and Beans 37
Beckenof 109
Beef:-
    Beef and Pepper Hash 100
    Fillet of Beef 98
    Fillet of Beef with Currants 98
    Home Alone Meat Loaf 117
    Steak with Mustard and Tarragon 99
Beer Dough 179
Beetroot:-
    Beetroot and Walnut Salad 30
    Cold Beetroot Soup 26
Bière. Tarte a la..... 207
Bigos (Polish Hunter's Stew) 123
Biscuits:-
    Auntie Freda's Chocolate Coconut
    Bars 193
    Cheese biscuits 206
    Oatcakes 193
    Shortbread 191
    Vicarage Flapjacks 192
Blackcurrant Soufflé 200
Braised Endive 30
Bran Fruit Loaf 184
Brandy Croissant Pudding 135
Bread:-
    Banana Bread 182
    Bran Fruit Loaf 184
    Beer Dough 179
    Bread and Butter Pudding 156
    Bread and Jam Fritters 178
    Bread Sandwich. 185
    Flo's 'After The Show' Bread
    Pudding 141
    Everest Bread 181
    Irish Bread 182

Malted Brown Loaf 183
Sandwiches 195
Toast 180
Broccoli:-
    Lasagnette Veneziana 49
Broth. Old Bill's... 21
Brownies 183
Brûlée:-
    Crème Brûlée 142
    Fruits Brûlés 154
Cabbage:-
    Sweet and Sour Cabbage 36
    Pork with Red Cabbage 107
Cakes:-
    Brownies 183
    Disgusting Upside Down Matza Coffee
    Cake 180
    Finnish Tosca Cake 188
    Gingerbread 184
    Ginger Cake 190
    Katrina's Apple Cake 140
    Lamingtons 186
    Luscious Lemon Curd Cake 187
    Mayoress Slices 194
    Moist Chocolate Cake 191
    My Grandmother's Vinegar Cake 188
    Orange Cake 192
    Passion Cake 150
    Polish Poppy Seed Cake 189
    Sour Cream Cake 143
    Toffee Crisp 195
    Vanilla Crescents 135
Camembert and Smoked Salmon
    Quiche 62
Casseroles and Stews:-
    A simple recipe for Pork 114
    Beckenof 109
    Bigos (Polish Hunter's Stew) 123
    Coriander Seafood Casserole 56
    Fish Stew 67
    Herbed Chicken Egusi Soup 82
    Irish Coddle 120
    Irish Stew 108
    Lazy Chicken Casserole 80
    Leek and Dumpling Casserole 172
    Lobster Creole 61
    Pigeons en cocotte 93

Pork Casserole 198
Rabbit Casserole 94
Shrewsbury Lamb 100
Sausages in red wine 122
Vegetable and Bacon Stew 129
Cauliflower:-
Sicilian Cauliflower Sauce with
Buccatini 48
Dandul 36
Celeriac:-
Celeriac and Potato Gratin
Dauphinois 35
Celeriac Remoulade 37
Celery:-
Mr Smith's Celery Soup 21
Cheese:-
Camembert and Smoked Salmon
Quiche 62
Cheese Biscuits 206
Cheese on Toast 124
Cheese Pastries 205
Cheese Scones 186
Cheese Soufflé 131
Festive Filo Pie 162
Four Cheeses Pasta 45
Goat's Cheese and Bacon Salad 31
Potato Cheese 165
Raclette 116
Sauted greens, goat cheese and olives
with penne 45
Spanakopita 168
Spinach with Blue Cheese and Pasta 42
Spinach and Curd Cheese Pie 127
Stilton Slice 206
Cheesecake:-
Apple Cheesecake 137
Islington Cheesecake 134
Lemon Cheesecake 145
CHICKEN AND GAME 76–94
Chicken:-
Baked Lemon Chicken 86
Bang Bang Chicken 84
Chicken in Mango and Ginger Sauce 81
Chicken With Fruit 87
Cold Chicken Pie 79
Coronation Chicken 89
Herbed Chicken Egusi Soup 82

Hot Chicken Salad 80
Lazy Chicken Casserole 80
Maize-fed Chicken with Garlic and
Lemon Sauce 84
Poulet Bleu 86
Sage Chicken 78
Special Lamb/Chicken Curry 103
Spicy Coconut Chicken 82
Supremes of Chicken with
Asparagus 78
Chilled Egg Mixture 14
Chocolate:-
Auntie Freda's Chocolate Coconut
Bars 193
Brownies 183
Chocolate Paté 210
Chocolate Soufflé 200
Crunchie Bar Ice cream 153
Lamingtons 186
Maud's Chocolate Pudding 144
Mayoress Slices 194
Moist Chocolate Cake 191
Slice of Heaven 209
The Ultimate Hot Chocolate 211
Tira-Me-Su 211
Chops:-
Lamb Chops St Paul's Road 102
Pork Chops with Soured Cream and
Mushrooms 109
Christmas:-
Christmas Salad 32
Mother's Christmas Pudding 152
Chutney:-
Tomato Chutney. Fish Kebabs with.... 71
Clafoutis. Fruits..... 155
Coconut:-
Auntie Freda's Chocolate Coconut
Bars 193
Lamingtons 186
Mayoress Slices 194
Spicy Coconut Chicken 82
Cod:-
Cod In Abbot Ale Batter 68
Kokt Torsk Med Senapsas (Steamed Cod
with Mustard Sauce) 70
Cod's Roe:-
Taramasalata 204

Cold Beetroot Soup 26
Cold Chicken Pie 79
Cold Scotch Woodcock 15
Consommé Mousse 14
Coppers' Concoction 59
Coriander:-
    Coriander Seafood Casserole 56
    Lamb Kebabs with Coriander
    Sauce 104
Corn Pudding 175
Coronation Chicken 89
Courgette:-
    Courgette and Prawn Quiche 128
    Courgette Pie 164
Crabmeat Mousse 12
Creole. Lobster.... 61
Crème Brûlée 142
Croissant:-
    Brandy Croissant Pudding 135
Crunchie Bar Ice Cream 153
Cullen Skink Soup 24
Curry:-
    Mackerel and Banana Curry 62
    Special Lamb/Chicken Curry 103
Cuttlefish:-
    Seppie con Nero 64
Damsons:-
    Dams Gin 212
Dandul 36
Dauphinois. Celeriac and Potato Gratin..... 35
Dough:-
    Beer Dough 179
    Empanada Gallega 118
Dressings:-
    Herby Vinaigrette Dressing 33
    Slimmer's French Dressing 35
Drinks:-
    Apple Wine 215
    Dams Gin 212
    French '75 213
    Morning Breakfast Juices 160
    Mulled Wine 214
    Sloe Gin 212
    The Ultimate Hot Chocolate 211
    White Wine Fruit Cup 214
Disgusting Upside Down Matza Coffee
Cake 180

Duck:-
    Duck Salad 88
    Plum Duck 88
Dumplings:-
    Leek and Dumpling Casserole 172
Dutch Apple Pie 144
Egg:-
    Cheese Souffle 131
    Chilled Egg Mixture 14
    Cold Scotch Woodcock 15
    Oeufs Marie Antoinette 13
    Piperade 115
    Scrambled Eggs and Bacon 126
Empanada Gallega 118
Endive:-
    Braised 30
Escarole:-
    Salad of hot potatoes, bacon, onions
    with Escarole 119
Everest Bread 181
Everton's Toffee 179
Ferrari's Pasta al Carcioli 53
Festive Filo Pie 162
Fillet of Beef 98
Fillet of Beef with Currants 98
Finnish Tosca Cake 188
FISH 54–74
Fish:-(see also Anchovy, Cod, Hake, etc.)
    Fish Kebabs with Tomato Chutney 71
    Fish Pasta 46
    Fish Stew 67
    Flat Fish Fillets with Prawns 74
    Graham's Fish Sauce 72
    Salmon Fishcakes 63
Flan de Poivrons 174
Flapjacks:-
    Vicarage Flapjacks 192
Flat Fish Fillets with Prawns 74
Flo's Delicious After the Show Bread
    Pudding 141
Fool:-
    Banana Fool 140
    Rhubarb Fool 137
Four Cheeses Pasta 45
French Dressing. Slimmer's..... 35
French Onion Soup 20
French '75 213

Frito Misto Mare 64
Fritters:-
  Bread and Jam fritters 178
Fruits Brulés 154
Fruits Clafoutis 155
Fudge:-
  Baked Fudge Pudding 143
  Nancy's Scottish Tablet 194
Game:-
  Gloucestershire Pheasant 90
  Guinea Fowl. Slow Cooked with
  Polenta..... 92
  Partridge in a Pot 91
  Pigeons en Cocotte 93
  Rabbit Casserole 94
Gazpacho 25
Gin:-
  Dams Gin 212
  Sloe Gin 212
Ginger:-
  Chicken in Mango and Ginger Sauce 81
  Ginger Cake 190
  Gingerbread 184
Gloucestershire Pheasant 90
Goat's Cheese:-
  Goat's Cheese and Bacon Salad 31
  Sauted greens, goat's cheese and olives
  with penne 45
Golden Vegetable Layer 168
Graham's Fish Sauce 72
Green Pea and Watercress Soup 23
Guinea Fowl with Polenta, slow
  cooked.... 92
Haddock:-
  Cullen Skink Soup 24
  Kedgeree 57
Hake:-
  The Upper Street Fish Shop Recipe for
  73
Herbed Chicken Egusi Soup 82
Herby Vinaigrette Dressing 33
Herring Roe:-
  Summer Pâté 200
Home Alone Meat Loaf 117
Homemade Baked Beans 34
Hot Chicken Salad 80
Humous 167

Ice cream:-
  Crunchie Bar Ice cream 153
  Mint Ice cream and Mint Sauce 149
Iced Watercress and Lemon Soup 17
Indian Pudding 148
Irish Bread 182
Irish Coddle 120
Irish Stew 108
Islington Cheesecake 134
Italian Sauce. All Purpose..... 43
Juniper berries:-
  Pork with Red Cabbage 107
Juices:-
  Morning breakfast juices 160
Kalamarakia Krassata 69
Katrina's Apple Cake 140
Kebabs:-
  Fish Kebabs with Tomato Chutney 71
  Lamb Kebabs with Coriander
  Sauce 104
Kedgeree 57
Kidneys:-
  Rognons Flambe with Saffron Rice
  106
Kokt Torsk Med Senapsas (Steamed Cod
  with Mustard Sauce) 70
Lamb:-
  Beckenof 109
  Irish Stew 108
  Lamb Chops St Paul's Road 102
  Lamb Kebabs with Coriander
  Sauce 104
  Sweetbreads in Sour Cream 126
  Persian Lamb Fillets 102
  Rognons Flambés with Saffron
  Rice 106
  Shrewsbury Lamb 100
  Special Lamb/Chicken Curry 103
  Tasty Leg of Lamb 101
Lamingtons 186
Lasagne:-
  Vegetable Lasagne 170
Lasagnette Veneziana 49
Lazy Chicken Casserole 80
Leeks:-
  Leek and Dumpling Casserole 172
  Leek and Potato Soup 17

Left-overs:-
  Beef and Pepper Hash 100
  Bigos (Polish Hunter's Stew) 123
  Pilaff 130
Lemon:-
  Baked Lemon Chicken 86
  Iced Watercress and Lemon Soup 17
  Lemon Cheesecake 145
  Lemon Delicious 151
  Lemon Soufflé 199
  Maize-fed Chicken with Garlic and
  Lemon Sauce 84
  Luscius Lemon Curd Cake 187
Lemon Sole:-
  Flat Fish Fillets with Prawns 74
Lobster Creole 61
Lot Au Chapeau 72
LUNCHES AND SUPPERS 113–131
Luscious Lemon Curd Cake 187
MacGregor's Athole Brose 139
Mackerel:-
  Mackerel and Banana Curry 62
  Smoked Mackerel Pâté 12
Maize-fed Chicken with Garlic and Lemon
  Sauce 84
Malted Brown Loaf 183
Mandarins:-
  Sour Cream Cake 143
Mangos:-
  Chicken in Mango and Ginger Sauce 81
Maud's Chocolate Pudding 144
Mayoress Slices 194
MEAT 96–111
Meat Loaf. Home Alone..... 117
Mediterranean Vegetables. Tagliatelle with
  Grilled..... 50
Mejillones a la Marinera 60
Michael's Mushrooms 205
Mincemeat:-
  Apple and Mincemeat Steam
  Pudding 151
Mint:-
  Mint Ice Cream and Mint Sauce 149
  Pea and Mint Soup 27
Moist Chocolate Cake 191
Monkfish:-
  Fish Stew 67

Lot Au Chapeau 72
Morning Breakfast Juices 160
Mother's Christmas Pudding 152
Mousse:-
  Consommé Mousse 14
  Crabmeat Mousse 12
  Mulberry Mousse 141
  Peach Mousse 150
  Salmon Mousse 12
  Mulberry Mousse 141
Mulled Wine 214
Mung Soup 24
Mushrooms:-
  Champignons Frederick's 15
  Festive Filo Pie 162
  Michael's Mushrooms 109
  Pork Chops with Sour Cream and
  Mushrooms 109
  Sweet and Spicy Mushrooms 163
  Three Mushroom Soup 18
Mussels:-
  Coppers' Concoction 59
  Fish Stew 67
  Mussels 58
  Mussels with White Wine and Garlic
  (Mejillones a la Marinera) 60
Mustard:-
  Steak with Mustard and Tarragon 99
  Swedish Mustard Sauce 66
  Kokt Torsk Med Senapsas (Steamed Cod
  with Mustard Sauce) 70
My Grandmother's Vinegar Cake 188
Nancy's Scottish Tablet 194
Oatcakes 193
Oeufs Marie Antoinette 13
Old Bill's Broth 21
Onions:-
  French Onion Soup 20
Olives:-
  Sauted greens, goat cheese and olives
  with penne 45
  Spanakopita 168
Orange Cake 192
Pancakes:-
  Coppers' Concoction 59
  Pig's Blood Pancakes 202

Parsnip:-
    Serendipitous Parsnip and Apple 167
GIVING A PARTY 196–215
Parties:-
    Party Puddings 199
    Supper Party for 20 198
Partridge In A Pot 91
Passion Cake 150
PASTA 40–53
Pasta:-
    Fish 46
    Pasta in Aubergine Sauce 52
    Pasta with a Raw Tomato Sauce 42
    Pasta with Sun-dried Tomatoes 52
    Poulet Bleu 86
    Seppie Con Nero 64
    Summerhouse Spicy Seafood Sauce 60
    Squid Salad with Pasta 48
    Vegetable Lasagne 170
Pastries:-
    Cheese Pastries 205
    Puff Pastry Yum Yum 149
Pâté:-
    Chocolate Pâté 210
    Smoked Mackerel Pâté 12
    Smoked Salmon Pâté 201
    Summer Pâté 200
Peaches:-
    Peach Mousse 150
Pea and Mint Soup 26
Peanut Soup 23
Pears:-
    Poached Pears with Two Sauces 136
Peas:-
    Favourite Pea recipes 33
    Green Pea and Watercress Soup 23
    Pea and Mint Soup 27
Peppers:-
    Beef and Pepper Hash 100
    Flan de Poivrons 174
    Pimientos a la Malagena 165
    Piperade 115
Persian Lamb Fillets 102
Pesto Alla Genovese 44
Pheasant:-
    Gloucestershire Pheasant 90
Pick Me Up:-
    Tira-Me-Su 211

Pies:-
    Aubergine Pie 161
    Cold Chicken Pie 79
    Courgette Pie 164
    Dutch Apple Pie 144
    Fabulous French Potato Pie 129
    Festive Filo Pie 162
    Savoury Sausage Pie 125
    Spinach and Curd Cheese Pie 127
Pigeons en Cocotte 93
Pig's Blood Pancakes 202
Pilaff 130
Pilaw Rice 169
Pimientos a la Malagena 165
Piperade 115
Plaice:-
    Flat Fish with Prawns 74
Plum Duck 88
Poached Pears with Two Sauces 136
Polenta:-
    Seppie Con Nero 64
    Slow Cooked Guinea Fowl with
    Polenta 92
Polish Poppy Seed Cake 189
Poor Man's Supper 120
Pork:-
    A Simple Recipe for Pork 114
    Beckenof 109
    Bigos (Polish Hunter's Stew) 123
    Empanade Gallega 118
    Pork Chops with Soured Cream and
    Mushrooms 109
    Pork Casserole 198
    Pork with Red Cabbage 107
    Pork with Sage 110
    Rillettes 121
    Roast Pork with Garlic 108
    Year Old Pig's Belly 111
Porridge:-
    Porridge 160
    Porridge and Humous 166
Potato Cheese (Himalayan) 165
Potato Pudding 173
Potatoes:-
    Celeriac and Potato Gratin
    Dauphinois 35
    Fabulous French Potatoe Pie 129

Leek and Potato Soup 17
Patatas Ala Importante 38
Potato Cheese (Himalayan) 165
Potato Pudding 173
Roast Garlic and Potato Soup 22
Salad of hot potatoes, bacon, onions
with Escarole 119
Poulet Bleu 86
POULTRY:-See Chicken and Game
Section 76–94
Duck Salad 88
Plum Duck 88
Prawns:-
A tip for Prawn Cocktails 20
Coppers' Concoction 59
Courgette and Prawn Quiche 128
Flat Fish with Prawns 74
Prawns and Pasta 46
PUDDINGS 132–156
Puddings:-
Apple and Mincemeat Steam
Pudding 151
Baked Fudge Pudding 143
Brandy Croissant Pudding 135
Bread and Butter Pudding 156
Flo's After the Show Bread
Pudding 141
Indian Pudding 148
Maud's Chocolate Pudding 144
Mother's Christmas Pudding 152
Puff Pastry Yum Yum 149
Quiche:-
Camembert and Smoked Salmon
Quiche 62
Courgette and Prawn Quiche 128
Rabbit Casserole 94
Raclette 116
Red Cabbage:-
Pork with Red Cabbage 107
Rhubarb Fool 137
Rice:-
Beef and Pepper Hash 100
Coriander Seafood Casserole 56
Kedgeree 57
Lobster Creole 61
Lot Au Chapeau 72
Persian Lamb Fillets 102

Pilaff 130
Pilaw 169
Pork with Sage 110
Rognons Flambés with Rice 106
Spicy Coconut Chicken 82
Stir-fried Scallops with Vegetables 68
West Indian Rice with Beans 37
Rillettes 121
Roast Garlic and Potato Soup 22
Roast Pork with Garlic 108
Rocket and Chilli Pasta 44
Rognons Flambés with Saffron Rice 106
Saffron:-
Rognons Flambés with Saffron
Rice 106
Sage:-
Pork with Sage 110
Sage Chicken 78
Salads:-
Aubergine and Tomatoes 38
Beetroot and Walnut Salad 30
Celeriac Remoulade 37
Christmas Salad 32
Duck Salad 88
Goat's Cheese and Bacon Salad 31
Hot Chicken Salad 80
Salade Composé au Saumon Fumé 202
Salade Cuite 32
Salad of Hot Potatoes, Bacon, Onions
with Escarole 119
Squid Salad 48
Tomato Herb Salad 30
SALADS AND VEGETABLES 28–39
Salmon:-
Camembert and Smoked Salmon
Quiche 62
Salad Composé au Saumon Fumé 202
Salmon Fishcake 63
Salmon Mousse 12
Smoked Salmon 16
Smoked Salmon Pâté 201
Sandwiches 195
Sauces:-
All-purpose Italian Sauce 43
Chicken in Mango and Ginger Sauce 81
Gloucestershire Pheasant 90
Graham's Fish Sauce 72

224

Kokt Torsk Med Senapses (Steamed Cod with Mustard Sauce) 70
Lamb Kebabs with Coriander Sauce 104
Maize-fed Chicken with Garlic and Lemon Sauce 84
Pasta in Aubergine Sauce 52
Poached Pears with Two Sauces 136
Pasta with Raw Tomato Sauce 42
Sicilian Cauliflower Sauce with Bucatini 48
Summerhouse Spicy Seafood Sauce 60
Swedish Mustard Sauce 66
Watercress Sauce 162
Sausages:-
  Bigos (Polish Hunter's Stew) 123
  Irish Coddle 120
  Sausages in Red Wine 122
  Savory Sausage Pie 125
  Toad in the Hole 122
Sauteed Greens, Goat Cheese and Olives with Penne 45
Savoury Sausage Pie 125
Scallops:-
  Fish Pasta 46
  Stir-fried Scallops with Vegetables 68
Scones:-
  Cheese Scones 186
  Wholemeal Scones 187
Scrambled Eggs and Bacon 126
Seppie Con Nero (Cuttlefish in Ink) 64
Serendipitous Parsnip and Apple 167
Shortbread 191
Shrewsbury Lamb 100
Sicilian Cauliflower Sauce with Bucatini 48
Slice of Heaven 209
Slimmer's French Dressing 35
Sloe Gin 212
Smoked Mackerel Pâté 12
Smoked Salmon 16
Smoked Salmon Pâté 201
Soufflé:-
  Cheese Souffle 131
  Party Puddings -Lemon, Apricot, Blackcurrant and Chocolate Soufflés 199–200

SOUPS AND STARTERS 10–27
Soups:-
  Cold Beetroot Soup 26
  Cullen Skink Soup 24
  French Onion Soup 20
  Iced Watercress and Lemon Soup 17
  Gazpacho 25
  Green Pea and Watercress Soup 23
  Leek and Potato Soup 17
  Mr Smith's Celery Soup 21
  Mung Soup 24
  Old Bill's Broth 21
  Pea and Mint Soup 27
  Peanut Soup 23
  Roast Garlic and Potato Soup 22
  Three Mushroom Soup 18
Sour Cream:-
  Pork Chops with Soured Cream and Mushrooms 109
  Sour Cream Cake 143
  Sweetbreads in Sour Cream 126
Spanakopita 168
Special Lamb/Chicken Curry 103
Spicy Coconut Chicken 82
Spicy Seafood Sauce. Summerhouse..... 60
Spinach:-
  Spanakopita 168
  Spinach and Curd Cheese Pie 127
  Spinach with Blue Cheese and Pasta 42
Squid:-
  Fish Stew 67
  Frito Misto Mare 64
  Kalamarakia Krassata 69
  Squid Salad with Pasta 48
  Stuffed Squid 66
Steak with Mustard and Tarragon 99
Stews:-see Casseroles and Stews
Stilton Slice 206
Stir-fried Scallops with Vegetables 68
Strawberry Tart 208
Sultana Sponge Tart 138
Summer Pâté 200
Sun-Dried Tomatoes with Pasta 52
Supper Party for 20 198
Supremes of Chicken with Asparagus 78
Swedish Mustard Sauce 66
Sweet and Sour Cabbage, 36

Sweet and Spicy Mushrooms 163
Sweetbreads in Sour Cream 126
Sweets:-
  Everton's Toffee 179
  Nancy's Scottish Tablet 194
  Toffee 178
Tabbouleh 173
Tagliatelle with Grilled Mediterranean
  Vegetables 50
Taramasalata 204
Tarragon:-
  Steak with Mustard and Tarragon 99
Tarte A La Bière 207
Tarte Tatin 153
Tarts:-
  Tarte A La Bière 207
  Strawberry Tarte 208
  Sultana Sponge Tart 138
  Tarte Tatin 153
Tasty Leg of Lamb 101
The Ultimate Hot Chocolate 211
The Upper Street Fish Shop Recipe for
  Hake 73
Three Mushroom Soup 18
Tip for Prawn Cocktail 20
Tira-Me-Su (Pick Me Up) 211
Toad In The Hole 122
Toast 180
Toffee:-
  Everton's Toffee 179
  Toffee 178
  Toffee Crisp 195
Tomatoes:-
  All-purpose Italian Sauce 43
  Aubergine and Tomatoes 38
  Flan de Poivrons 174
  Gazpacho 25
  Lasagnette Veneziana 49
  Pasta with Raw Tomato Sauce 42
  Pasta with Sun-dried Tomatoes 52
  Salad Cuite 32
  Tomato Chutney 71
  Tomato Herb Salad 30
Vanilla Crescents 135
Vegetable and Bacon Stew 129
Vegetable Lasagne 170
Vegetable Pasta 53

Vegetables:- (see also artichoke, courgette,
  potatoes, etc.)
  Tagliatelle with Grilled Mediterranean
  Vegetables 50
  Stir-fried Scallops with Vegetables 68
  Vegetable and Bacon Stew 129
  Vegetable Lasagne 170
  Vegetable Layer. Golden..... 168
  Vegetable Pasta 53
VEGETARIAN 159–175
Vegetarian dishes:-
  Courgette Pie 164
  Fabulous French Potato Pie 129
  Ferrari's Pasta al Carcioli 53
  Four Cheeses Pasta 45
  Lasagnette Veneziana 49
  Pasta with Raw Tomato Sauce 42
  Pasta with Sun-dried Tomatoes 52
  Pesto alla Genovese 44
  Piperade 115
  Rocket and Chilli Pasta 44
  Sauted greens, goat cheese and olives
  with penne 45
  Sicilian Cauliflower Sauce with Bucatini 48
  Spinach with Blue Cheese and Pasta 42
  Spinach and Curd Cheese Pie 127
  Tagliatelle with Grilled Mediterranean
  Vegetables 50
  Vegetable Pasta 53
Vicarage Flap-Jacks 192
Vinaigrette Dressing. Herby..... 33
Vinegar Cake. My Grandmother's..... 188
Walnuts:-
  Beetroot and Walnut Salad 30
Watercress:-
  Watercress and Green Pea Soup 23
  Watercress and Lemon Soup. Iced..... 17
  Watercress Sauce 162
West Indian Rice and Beans 37
White Wine Fruit Cup 214
Wholemeal Scones 187
Wine:-
  Apple Wine 215
  French '75 213
  Mulled Wine 214
  White Wine Fruit Cup 214
Year Old Pig's Belly 111

The NSPCC Islington Cook Book is available by mail order, please send order form to NSPCC Trading Co Ltd, P O Box 934, Poole, Dorset BH17 7BR

All proceeds from the sale of this book will go to the National Society for the Prevention of Cruelty to Children.

Please send me ..... copies at £7.50 each

postage and packing £   2.50

Enclosed is an additional donation to the NSPCC £_____

Total enclosed: £_____

Send to: PLEASE USE CAPITAL LETTERS

Title (Mr/Mrs Ms etc)

Name

Address

Postcode   Tel. No

Signature

Make cheques payable to Marketing Matters Ltd.
(please add your address on the back).

Access/Visa card no. | | | | | | | | | | | | | | | | | | | |

Expiry date

For further information and Credit Card orders please telephone 0202 669940.
Please allow 21 days for delivery.

Charity Registration No. 216401